LANDMARKS IN LITERATURE

Maynard Mack, *Series Editor*
Yale University

Some books belong to all times and places. They are the rivers, mountains, seas, and continents of our intellectual and moral world. They tell us where we are and how far we have still to go. They are, in short, our landmarks.

Landmarks in Literature is a series of interpretive studies of such books, each written by an authority of today, each a reference point between our present and our past.

LISELOTTE DIECKMANN, author of this volume in the Landmarks in Literature series, received her Ph.D. from Heidelberg University in 1927. She has been Professor of German and Comparative Literature at Washington University, St. Louis since 1959, and has served on the Executive Council of the Modern Language Association. She has written many articles on symbolism in literature, and is the author of *Hieroglyphics—The History of a Literary Symbol* and of a forthcoming book on Goethe.

5636103
832|GOE

DIECKMANN, L. | GOETHE'S
FAUST.

Please renew/return this item by the last date shown.

So that your telephone call is charged at local rate, please call the numbers as set out below:

	From Area codes 01923 or 0208:	From the rest of Herts:
Renewals:	01923 471373	01438 737373
Enquiries:	01923 471333	01438 737333
Minicom:	01923 471599	01438 737599

Hertfordshire
COUNTY COUNCIL
Community Information

2 0 MAR 2004

3 0 NOV 2009

CENTRAL RESOURCES
LIBRARY
01707 281530

L32a

GOETHE'S *FAUST*

A CRITICAL READING

❦

LISELOTTE DIECKMANN

PRENTICE-HALL, INC., ENGLEWOOD CLIFFS, N.J.

COUNTY
COPY

HERTFORDSHIRE
COUNTY LIBRARY
832 GoE
5636103

Copyright © 1972 by Prentice-Hall, Inc., *Englewood Cliffs, New Jersey.*
All rights reserved. No part of this book may be reproduced in any form
or by any means without permission in writing from the publisher. ISBN:
O-13–357731–7. *Library of Congress Catalog Card Number 70–175516.*
Printed in the United States of America.

10 9 8 7 6 5 4 3 2 1

PRENTICE-HALL INTERNATIONAL, INC. (*London*)
PRENTICE-HALL OF AUSTRALIA, PTY. LTD. (*Sydney*)
PRENTICE-HALL OF CANADA, LTD. (*Toronto*)
PRENTICE-HALL OF INDIA PRIVATE LIMITED (*New Delhi*)
PRENTICE-HALL OF JAPAN, INC. (*Tokyo*)

✌§ PREFACE §✎

This book is written for the reader already acquainted with *Faust,*
at least in a cursory fashion. It is not meant as an introduction to an
unknown work, but rather as an interpretation of a puzzling work
that needs more than one reading to be absorbed.

In most cases I have used the translation by John Shawcross (London: Allan Wingate Ltd., 1959), because it imitates Goethe's meters
and rhymes faithfully while at the same time making the meaning
clear. However, as this translation is hard to find, I have indicated
the line numbers of the original German, so that the reader may
use any other translation available. At times I have preferred the
translation by Charles E. Passage (Indianapolis: The Bobbs-Merrill
Company, Library of Liberal Arts, 1965). These passages are indicated by adding (P) after the line numbers.

I owe very special thanks to Professor Maynard Mack of Yale University who, with the patience of an angel and the critical stamina
of a man, helped to organize my chaotic manuscript.

◄§ CONTENTS §►

V. THE PLOT

GOETHE'S *FAUST*

A CRITICAL READING

❧ I ❧

INTRODUCTION

THE GENESIS OF GOETHE'S FAUST

The theme of a man who sells his soul to the devil to gain knowledge, power, riches, and pleasure, existed as early as the beginning of Christianity. It rose from an ascetic attitude toward life and a profound faith in life after death. Seen from this religious viewpoint, a desire for these earthly satisfactions must indeed have seemed the product of a pact with the devil.

Under various names the story is told in late antiquity and during the Middle Ages. The Renaissance added its newly awakened desire for secular knowledge which, not yet able to find satisfaction in what we now call natural science, frequently turned to the practice of magic and alchemy. At this period the legend became attached to the name of Faustus, which means, the fortunate one. The German chapbook, *Historia von Dr. Johann Fausten*, published in Frankfurt in 1587, is the first complete printed account of a legendary pact made by a certain Dr. Faustus with the devil, reporting his remarkable life—in which he displays both great intellectual curiosity and idle attempts at gaining power through magic tricks—as well as his terrible death, a story clearly intended as a warning to the reader not to follow in his footsteps. Christopher Marlowe based his play on an English version of this German book. In his play the search for knowledge is soon perverted into empty magic tricks, and Faust dies at the end of his allotted time, a victim of the devil whom he had preferred to the saving voices of men and angels.

1

Goethe read Marlowe only late in his life. His own inspiration came from the various puppet plays derived from the chapbook which were popular in Germany and which added, for the amusement of the audience, the comic figure Hanswurst, who, like some of Marlowe's buffoons, constantly interrupts the serious course of events. In the conception of his "devil" Mephistopheles, Goethe included and vastly enlarged upon this comic element.

By the second half of the eighteenth century, when Goethe started working on *Faust,* life on earth was no longer held up to scorn. Knowledge, power, wealth, and pleasure were no longer considered temptations of satanic powers, and nobody could write a wholesale condemnation of them without being open to ridicule. In the climate of thought of the late eighteenth century most great Western ideas underwent profound changes; concepts such as truth, good and evil, art and its function, even the transience of life were seen in a new light. To write a modern *Faust,* the poet had to reinterpret every meaning that made the older *Faust* plays moving and poignant. Thus, Goethe changed the devil into an ironic figure, handled knowledge, wealth, and power satirically, added an extensive love story, and allowed Faust's soul to be saved in the end. He also added for poetic reasons a large amount of mythological material, only a fraction of which occurs in any of the older versions. In short, he wrote a modern reinterpretation of the ancient legend.

A first, very incomplete prose version of the play was written during Goethe's youthful *Sturm und Drang* period, but remained unpublished in his lifetime.[1] Some years later he struggled with the work again, and in 1789 published a *Fragment.* It was only years later, after considerable pressure from his friend Schiller, that he found a conception of the whole to which he could adhere, more or less, until he finished the work in its present form shortly before his death in 1832. Almost sixty years of life, of experience and experiment had thus gone into it. Its slow development allowed the author not only to suffuse it with his own mature thoughts and feelings, but to develop a language for it that gained immeasurably from his poetic maturity. The young Goethe could not have written the language that the aging Faust speaks, whereas the old Goethe was entirely capable of finding rapturous, youthful tones. We may put this differently: As the author matured he was able to achieve the poetic detachment which alone makes a work of art great. He manipulated words and characters without identifying with them, and handled his material with increasing objectivity. In the final version of the play the conscious hand of the artist is felt throughout, and the play of the poetic imagination is free of subjective impulses.

When Goethe finally felt ready in 1808 to publish Part I of the work he was almost sixty years of age. He had greatly changed the original and had planned and partly written Part II. At that time of his life the entire concept was in his mind, and both Parts I and II are accordingly held together by a unified idea of the whole which he carried out over the next twenty years with very minor modifications. Let us consider first the nature of this unified conception.

CRITICAL APPROACH

During its nearly one hundred forty years of existence, the work has been viewed by critics in diverse and contradictory ways—from enthusiastic praise to almost complete condemnation, with every shade of evaluation in between. The German bourgeois society of the nineteenth and early twentieth centuries, proud of its great national poet, was too overwhelmed by his "greatest work" to allow a critical attitude to arise. Faust was praised for his unceasing striving and for his final achievement of an ideal society; his ultimate redemption was seen as the logical consequence of his own deserving actions. Outside of Germany, too, most approaches were reverential.

In due course, a different attitude made itself felt. Two fundamental objections have been raised, one concerning the hero, the other the form of the work—both so obvious to an unbiased reader that it is hard to understand why they were developed so late. The objection to the hero is grave. Faust's restless striving, so the argument runs, is a very complex response to human experience, and leads, among other questionable actions, to the murder of his beloved Gretchen's brother and indirectly to the murder of her mother and her child, as well as to her own execution. In *Faust* Part II, it leads to the death of an old couple, Philemon and Baucis, to the production of worthless paper money at the Emperor's court, and to a more than questionable victory over the enemy's army. All of this in the name of highest aspirations. The nature of Faust's final redemption becomes obscure when the hero can no longer be considered a "good" man.

The objection to the form of the work is equally grave. Many critics no longer consider *Faust* an accomplished work of art, but rather a haphazard product of too many years of interrupted composition, lacking a unified structure as well as a unified style. It is not effective drama, they point out, but is couched in a form inappropriate to its content and meaning. Responding to these objections, recent criticism has attempted to rescue the play and its hero from a devaluation felt to be just as misleading as was the earlier praise. We now have enough historical distance from the author to judge the work with less prejudice than former generations, and we can see now—almost, I think, for the first time—to what extent both form and character foreshadow "modern" forms and "modern" man.

The unsteady seeker of a truth he will never find, the sceptical, critical, dissatisfied, and insatiable protagonist is less a romantic hero, as Santayana[2] considered him to be, than a modern man who has lost faith in religion, philosophy, human relationships, and many other supports dear to human beings. Faust is an isolated and, in a modern sense, alienated person, in many ways closer to Camus's existential hero in *The Fall* than to his contemporary romantic brothers. To call his way through life a quest for truth is unduly stretching the concept of truth. On the other hand, he does make *some* sort of way through life, and to unravel its meaning will be our task in these pages.

The poetic form Goethe found for his theme was likewise new. It marked a radical break with classical forms and Aristotelian poetics. When the work was published in its complete form in 1831, the romantic period was almost over and the so-called symbolistic school of literature was soon to be heard from. *Faust* is in fact the first symbolistic work. In the past twenty years scholars have begun to realize this and have addressed themselves to such essential questions as the function of the characters within the work, the role of language, meter, rhyme, the pervasive symbolism and imagery. The meaning of *Faust* is now finally seen to exist in the interrelationship of all these elements, to be inseparably linked to them and not to be extractable in the form of independent, philosophic statements. It follows from what has been said that to understand the work, an approach must be used which will correspond to Goethe's intentions. In this type of literature, plot and character are subordinate to the poetic statement of the whole and not to be isolated from the constituent poetic elements just mentioned. Many things in the play which seem absurd when seen from a merely realistic point of view will become meaningful in a symbolic context.

Our discussion must start with a few generalizations. These are not the customary "ideas" normally abstracted from *Faust*. Rather they are the philosophic presuppositions of the entire work, which it is helpful to understand in advance of the reading. It should be emphasized that these generalizations are not expressed by Goethe as ideas or themes. On the contrary, the work has a great power of poetic transformation; its ideas and themes exist in fact only as visual or auditory experiences. The work appeals to our aesthetic imagination rather than to our discursive reasoning. In the discussion of the ideas presented, I will therefore turn to the artistic form in which they actually appear. I have chosen my examples arbitrarily, and it should be understood that other examples could be used without disturbing the conclusions. In the symbolistic technique of the whole, each example is only a mirror of the idea, and any number of such mirrors occur in the work. It will be the reader's task to supplement these examples by others.

Building on the presuppositions of the work, which are discussed in the next chapter, Chapters III and IV analyze the modes and forms of poetic presentation. The interaction between form and meaning is so compact in *Faust* that in almost all instances elements of form will help to elucidate thought. To force a wedge between them destroys that essential tension between the idea and its poetic expression which is the most outstanding aspect of the drama. Having established essential guidelines on how to read the work, I proceed in Chapter V to discuss the plot and to attempt a consistent interpretation, placing particular emphasis on the connections that exist between the two parts of the work, with respect to themes, poetic devices, mythological material, and related elements.

⤳ II ⤳

PHILOSOPHIC PRESUPPOSITIONS

LIFE ON EARTH

The fundamental purpose of *Faust* is to represent, in a work of art, man's place within the confines of life on this earth, more specifically biological and physical life. At the end of the eighteenth century, as faith in Christian doctrine was waning and knowledge of the natural sciences rising, this was a burning concern, and *Faust* explores the radical changes demanded by the new orientation. By "biological" I mean not only the possibilities and limitations imposed on every human being by his biological constitution and his psychological and emotional drives and urges, but also the growth and decay of plant and animal life. By "physical" I understand the nonbiological aspects of nature, such as the movements of clouds, wind, water, rock formations, mountains, light and darkness, the whole realm of nonliving nature in which life is placed.

The poem constitutes a modern scientific view of life, a relentless effort to explore man's potential and limitations within the natural laws to which he is subjected. Except for Diderot's *Rêve de D'Alembert*, which is concerned with the physiological aspects of man's nature, I know no literary work of the eighteenth or early nineteenth century which grapples with this truly fundamental problem in the same searching way.

This scientific concept of life, although underlying the whole work, is constantly transformed into poetic vision. Goethe's relationship to nature does not rest upon vague romantic emotions, but rather

7

on scientific inquiry and productive research as far as they were within his reach. The scientific vision of life offered to the poet not only the intellectual and emotional problems with which Faust must come to terms, but simultaneously a wealth of "natural" imagery and symbolism. Life on earth is thus not only an intellectual, but at every moment also a poetic concern. The fusion of the two approaches, or better the transformation of the scientific approach into poetry, forms the fabric of the work.

There is, however, in *Faust* a third approach to "life on earth" which, while close to the poetic aspect, stands in a somewhat uneasy relationship to the purely scientific one. Goethe tries to integrate concepts of evolution, metamorphosis, the flow of time, and so on, into a neo-Platonic framework. He is by no means a mystic, but the neo-Platonic idea of a world-soul from which life emanates and to which it ultimately returns appeals to him as an image of the overall harmony into which our unharmonious life on earth might finally resolve. To be sure, the comparative vagueness of this neo-Platontic notion enabled him to set Faust's life in a philosophic superstructure without forcing him to abandon his modern scientific outlook. In many of his late poems, in which he praises the ever creative force of the world-soul, Goethe conveys the feeling that this is less a matter of faith or religion than of poetic vision. The same holds true for *Faust*. But, as we shall see, the seams holding together an ancient belief and a modern biological attitude become at times visible. The twentieth-century reader may wish that Goethe had not needed to superimpose upon his harsh view of life on earth the calm and harmonious vision with which he begins and ends.

Time and the Transformation of Forms

In one decisive respect, the neo-Platonic outlook confirms the harsh view. If, as the neo-Platonists believed, life is considered to be a series of emanations issuing from and striving to return to the living godhead, it follows that everything, living or nonliving, is in a state of continuous flux and change. Into no other philosophical framework, therefore, could Goethe so readily have fitted his grand understanding of life as change, motion, and transformation. The work vibrates with a vitality that can find no satisfaction in any static situation. Physical and biological life move and change in a ceaseless motion similar in its endless variety to that in which Faust's own outward as well as inner life moves. Man is no longer the center of the universe; rather, he is one part, perhaps an important one, of that sweeping motion and flux which is the essence of life. Goethe set himself the task of exploring to the fullest the terrifying as well as the beneficial consequences of this eternal natural motion and change.

The endless flow of both his biological and his inner life is a deeply disturbing feature for a man like Faust who earnestly attempts to find permanent values. Permanence is by necessity absent. Faust's ever present uneasiness is largely due to the paradox that there exist in the human mind ideas of durability and permanence which find, neither in nature nor in the life of man, a true correspondence.

The paradox inherent in this view of life can be expressed as the simultaneous presence in our minds of constant form and continual change. To cite a simple example, we may think of the apparently permanent form of a leaf which, as we know, undergoes a constant process of change. Goethe was throughout his life acutely aware of this problem, and it becomes Faust's own. As he longs and searches for something lasting, for a form that does not vanish, only to discover again and again the essentially transitory quality of all his experiences, Faust despairs. And yet the reader, knowing Faust to be as mutable as everything around him, realizes that even this state of despair has no permanence and that the inner logic of the play demands of him a continuing search in which despair will alternate with hope.

In nature, the flow of time expresses itself not only in alternation and development, but specifically in what Goethe calls metamorphosis. His favorite examples, which he often uses as symbols for man's own changes, are the butterfly developing from the chrysalis and the leaf unfolding from its bud. He also likes, as a metaphor of man's changes, the image of death and rebirth.

In the action of the play, moreover, both Faust and Mephistopheles sometimes change appearances: Faust is rejuvenated in the Witches' Kitchen, and in Act III he is transformed into a medieval lord. Mephistopheles appears as a female monster in the same act, and elsewhere enjoys his several disguises as a scholar. The little Homunculus, too, dies and is reborn. In short, the play's foremost concern is to give a sensory form to abstract ideas of motion and change.

REALITY AND ILLUSION

The problem of form and change leads immediately to a related problem. A reality that rapidly changes leaves the onlooker with the suspicion that what he just experienced was not "real" in the first place, but rather an illusion of his mind or senses. For Faust every experience turns into an illusion as reality recedes. This is true for sense impressions as well as for intellectual and emotional experiences. Faust has a keen awareness of the evasiveness of reality, which seems to show him its illusory rather than its "real" character.

This painful situation is considerably enhanced by the fact that Faust is basically a dreamer; in other words, he has a strong tendency to let his imagination encroach upon reality. When he then turns to reality he finds it disillusioning because it does not correspond to his dream. Thus, as he sees the sun setting on his Easter walk, he daydreams that he will always follow it—"before me the day and behind the night"—whereas in reality the sun sets and leaves him in darkness. On other occasions he has actual dreams, for example, the one sent to him by Mephistopheles's spirit servants. This dream of beautiful landscapes is illusory at two levels. Not only does it disappear when he awakens, it is created so that the devil may escape while he is asleep. Faust has many additional dreams, presented either as daydreams or nighttime experiences.

Their significance depends upon the particular situation in which they occur, but all help immerse him in an illusory world so that he is eternally haunted by the problem: "What is real?" [3]

The poet's own awareness of the illusory character of reality on the other hand produces the very means of his art. Goethe himself has complete mastery over the realities and illusions he intends to create. The story of *Faust,* with its magic and its disregard for time and place, was ideally suited for the creation of poetic illusions, and the author makes it abundantly clear that he is not dealing with "realistic" settings, characters, or events. Spirits appear throughout, ancient monsters have stage reality, magic tricks are played, and most of the inhabitants of the spirit world meet in a "northern" or "classical" Walpurgisnight. Stage effects, such as the creation and extinction of artificial fire, are carefully handled to intensify the illusory environment.

The emphasis on illusion creates in the poem a dual perspective. On the one hand its protagonist is the ardent seeker of a reality which disillusions him. On the other hand its author finds in illusion a true realm of art which is ever the source of joy. In the tension rising from the treatment of illusion as both a higher artistic reality and as the unreality experienced by Faust lies much of the power of the work.

DUALISM AND THE RHYTHM OF LIFE

The contrasts between illusion and reality and between form and change make up the fundamental rhythm according to which the play functions. In some ways this rhythm corresponds to the rhythm of life itself. Inhaling and exhaling, growing and decaying, living and dying—these constitute, as Goethe frequently emphasizes, the "natural rhythm" of life. In man, moreover, with his intellectual and emotional self-awareness, these natural polarities lead on to much more complex opposites, contradictions, and paradoxes, all of them producing tensions either within the mind, or between the mind and its environment, or between two minds. In the first scene of the work the angels, who as spirits are not affected by inner tensions, give to the audience an overall view of the earth. From their vantage point they see the planet's endless rotation and point out the alternation of day and night. Thus the audience is prepared for opposites from the very first lines of the work, and will be exposed to them up to and including the very last scene.

In Faust himself, the rhythm of day and night symbolizes the struggle between biological desire and spiritual aspiration. He calls these inner forces his higher and lower soul, and suffers from the conflict they create in him. This dualism is further complicated by the existence of Mephistopheles, who always takes the side of Faust's lower soul. He compares mankind

> To our long-legged friend
> the grasshopper,
> who ever flits and springs,
> and springs and flits,
> then sings his ancient song,
> while in the grass he sits.
> (288–90)

This is the devil's view of the human conflict; since he stands outside of it he will never experience its agonizing reality. For Faust, on the other hand, this reality is the essence of his existence. In contrast to Mephistopheles, for whom high aspirations are not within reach, Faust soars high only to feel thwarted by his lower instincts, which he curses but is not able to overcome. Caught in the dualism of his own nature, Faust experiences this conflict as the basic condition of man.

Faust's experiences are thus subject to two entirely opposed viewpoints, and the same is true for all other occurrences in the play. Whatever he views with delight or approval the devil considers worthless. Whatever pleases the devil, *he* considers worthless. This is an antagonism that Faust often strongly expresses, whereas Mephistopheles, never emotionally involved, smilingly allows his partner to chafe under it.

To emphasize these contrasts Goethe alternates comic and serious scenes so that the reader can never relax in one mood. Just as Faust is driven through his life by conflicting desires, so the reader is teased throughout the play by an alternating rhythm of seriousness and comedy. Up to the very last scene the devil always adds a final mocking word. Only after he himself is exposed to ridicule by the angels are we allowed to forget him and to concentrate on what will happen to Faust's "immortal part." In the end, but only in the end, the dualism between seriousness and mockery ceases to exist and the rhythm of laughter and tears subsides.

The alternation of the comic and the serious is one of many examples which show how the form of the work expresses its meaning. For the main structural characteristic of Faust is the presence of a dialectic which consists of thesis and antithesis without synthesis. Nothing in the flow of life and time is ever resolved. The two sides of each situation are, although always presenting only a limited aspect, always both valid. The rare moments of the play where we believe we are witnessing momentary solutions give way quickly to new events, new hopes, and new downfalls. Life on earth and man's awareness of it, according to Goethe, are not open to solutions. He has chosen a dialectical form which corresponds to his vision of the two sides of human existence.

ᵉᶳ III ᶳᵉ

MODES OF PRESENTATION

SYMBOLISM

An author who wants to present a man's life on earth might choose to do this by "realistic" means such as we find in most nineteenth-century novels. This was not at all Goethe's intent. Instead, he wrote a highly imaginative work, making full use of the fantastic possibilities of the subject matter. He tied his fantastic material to reality, however, by making the real as well as the imaginary material symbolic. Almost as in a medieval work, the reader has to be alert simultaneously to the immediate literal significance and to the larger symbolic reference of every passage. In the following pages I give some examples of this symbolistic technique.

Goethe's symbolism in *Faust*, though taken from nature like that of most other poets of his time, has a distinguishing character. In the first place, the nature images are almost always dynamic, that is, nature is shown in motion and flux. It is neither static nor picturesque. Almost every image and symbol can be shown to express some sort of motion, change, or development. In the second place, Goethe was very specially attracted to water in all forms. Its ever-changing quality, its perpetual motion, the fact that it is a life-giving force—all combined to make it his favorite source of images and symbols. Thus Thales can say to the ocean:

> Everything out of water began!
> Everything does the water sustain!
> Ocean, grant us your ceaseless reign!

> Were there no clouds by you outspread,
> Were no rich brooklets by you fed,
> Nor rivers down their courses sped,
> Nor streams brimmed full bed after bed,
> Where would our world be, or mountain, or plain?
> It is you who the freshness of life still maintain.
>
> (8436–42)   (P)

Goethe is particularly aware of the natural cycle of water.[4] As it evaporates over the ocean, moves in clouds back to the land, falls as rain, collects to form springs and rivers, and flows back to the ocean, water affords an ideal image of the neo-Platonic world-soul, which similarly emanates into matter and then returns to itself. When Goethe, for instance, uses the waterfall as an image of man's life, he is fully aware of its "falling" quality within this cycle.

Another favorite source of imagery for Goethe is the neo-Platonic analogy between the sun and God (or mind, truth, etc.), and the changes from light to darkness and from darkness to light which reflect the condition of man. The dualism in Faust's own life, as was said earlier, is expressed in this imagery. Goethe connects it symbolically with dualism of body and mind and uses it as a central image linking physical and spiritual life. Two striking examples of this symbolism may be seen in the first and last scenes in which Faust appears on stage. Both of these scenes are entitled "Night." The first is preceded by the angelic scene mentioned above, which is bathed in light; the last is followed by a light scene in which Faust's immortal part is carried upward. Thus the beginning and the end of Faust's life are set off on stage to symbolize his dark corporeal position on earth in sharp contrast to the scenes of brightness. This symbolism pervades the entire work. Even the devil understands it when he says to Faust: "Your lives alone by day and night are dated" (1784).

The work as a whole is written in clusters, or, to use one of Goethe's own terms, "tapestries" of symbols.[5] Gold is such a complex symbol. It is a negative symbol because it is a destructive force. Whenever Faust needs gold, Mephistopheles has to procure it, whether as a present for Margaret or as the hidden treasure on whose presumed existence the Emperor bases his paper money. Gold is also connected with the volcanic eruption that disturbs the serenity of the Classical Walpurgisnight, just as it is seen in the veins of the Hartz Mountain in the first Walpurgisnight. It causes strife, war, and destruction wherever it is wanted, and falls therefore naturally under the dominion of Mephistopheles. In the Masquerade scene, when Faust disguised as Plutus displays gold, it turns into flames, expressing the court's greed and the illusory quality of possessions in general.

Another symbolic arrangement is that which Goethe himself called "mirror reflection." Faust is reflected in a number of figures such as the Boy-Charioteer, Homunculus, Euphorion, Lynceus, each of them indicating and elucidating one facet of Faust's character. The mirror image of a woman that Faust sees in the Witches' Kitchen appears in the play as Gretchen, Helen, Galatea, Mary. The women themselves are in turn reflected in cloud formations. (See the beginning of Act IV.) Such reflections occur also for objects and events. The sun is reflected in the rainbow; water reflects life. Goethe has placed a large number of such "mirrors" in the work, bewildering us perhaps by their multiplicity, but orienting us unerringly toward the themes, characters, and events which they reflect.

MYTH

The symbolistic treatment of the work makes it possible for the author to use as symbols both "real" and "mythological" characters and events. The Margaret scenes are a good example of this mixture since Goethe made a special effort to make her appear "real." Not only is she fully human, but in the events of her life preceding her encounter with Faust, time, place and causality are clearly indicated. We are in a "neighbor's garden," the time is evening, and the reason for her visit to the neighbor is that she has found in her room a little treasure chest of unknown origin which has no place in her regular, well-ordered life.

The chest, however, introduces Margaret to a new dimension of existence: It is on the instigation and with the help of the devil that

Faust has put the chest in her room. And though her neatly ordered mind senses a mystery, her life has no defense against "demonic" forces. Thus a "mythological mode" is superimposed on her "realistic" existence and the union of the two modes of perception and presentation produces her bewilderment and ultimately her tragedy.

Myth, of which in *Faust* the demonic is part, is the creative poetic force that holds the work together. For *Faust* is not only a myth in its entirety; it is composed of myths and these are only partly of Goethe's own creation. They come from many worlds—classical, Germanic, Christian, neo-Platonic—and are intermingled freely with "real" characters. Thus Homunculus, whose origins lie in the neo-Platonic mysticism of the Renaissance, represents on a mythological level a modern view of evolution, and the marriage between the "real" Faust and the "mythological" Helen becomes a myth of art. All characters in the play are in fact equally real, regardless of their mythological features, since reality is measured only in terms of poetic reality. Hence, the monsters of the Classical Walpurgisnight appear more substantial and significant than the "real" characters at the Emperor's court who have to act out a masquerade in order to feel that they exist. The one standard applicable to all characters is that of poetic effectiveness.

Among the many myths on which the play draws, there is one which is disturbingly often taken to be part of the philosophical meaning of the work, though actually it is part of the mythological structure. This is the world of Christianity, which appears from beginning to end. Literally the Lord is present in the Prologue in Heaven, just as the Queen of Heaven is present in the last scene. There are moreover Christian scenes and references throughout. The mere existence of a devil is of course a sign of the presence of a Christian world.

This Christian world is treated, in agreement with the general polar rhythm of the work, in two entirely different ways—positive and negative. Negatively, the Christian world is not mythological: The many direct quotations from the Bible used by Goethe himself as marginal notes or spoken by the main characters are intended to be blasphemy. Particularly frequent are references to the Trinity, which, in each case, is blasphemously represented to be worldly, illusory, or devilish.[6] Plutus-Faust's words to the Boy-Charioteer (5628) are likewise blasphemous—"Beloved Son, in thee I am well pleased"—signaling at the very least a moment of outrageous hubris. Positively, on the other hand, Christian doctrines are treated as myth—though myths with universal appeal: The idea of a human Mother of God or the resurrection of Christ from the grave may move an unbeliever as much as a believer. Their hopeful promise is in fact the point for which Goethe uses them.

To be sure, these Christian scenes are not arbitrarily chosen. They are a natural and important part of the Faust legend, and, given Goethe's inclination to keep his hero in his original sixteenth-century environment, he must include the religion in which Faust was raised and from which he broke away. But within the frame of Goethe's work, they have no Christian meaning. The author does not aim, as the chapbook does, at Christian propaganda. The Christian imagery is simply a mythical setting for the hero's life and thought.

The case is only apparently different for the neo-Platonism that pervades the work. To be sure, Goethe longed in his youth to commune through nature with a world-soul. Even in his later years he kept a vision, however sober and restrained, of an all-pervasive life force, and continued to visualize this force as an animating world-spirit. But this was always less a philosophical than a mythical view. In fact, the neo-Platonic myth is the central myth of the work: The soul enters the body, suffers from the burden of the body, and happily returns to its source after death.[7]

Intricately related to this body of neo-Platonic myth, but expanded by Goethe into a rich and separate mythology, is the world of magic, involving the innumerable spirits and demons who surround Faust throughout his life. The figures of the first Walpurgisnight and of the Witches' Kitchen are by and large of Goethe's invention. Those of the second Walpurgisnight he took from ancient, rarely quoted sources, but transformed them into creatures of his own. The grand irony of the second or Classical Walpurgisnight is that, while its characters are taken from antiquity (although certainly not from classical Greek literature), they are re-shaped to transmit Goethe's very modern "myth" of evolution. All of these figures mingle easily in the poem with historical personages, who, in turn, receive a mythological coloring from their context, and all of them must be considered, ultimately, to be projections of Faust's own inner drives and subconscious forces.

Mythology is the pervasive mode of *Faust,* and as with all my-thology, its truth is suspended between reality and fantasy.

TIME, SPACE, CAUSALITY

Goethe's effort to present life as flux finds expression in the fact that nothing in the play is static; scenes, characters, natural events are presented on the stage in constant motion. Sometimes this mo-tion is described, as when Faust tells us of the sunrise at the begin-ning of Part II (4686–703): first the gradual change, occurring be-fore the sun appears, from plain light to varying colors, then the coursing of the sunlight from peaks to valley, where it finally hits Faust's eyes directly. Similar techniques are used to describe move-ments of characters and events on the stage wherever they are too complex to be visually presented to the audience.[8] Sometimes the motion is incorporated in stage directions:

> (Girl players, young and pretty, join the crowd: confidential talk is heard. Fishers and bird-catchers, with nets, rods and snares, come for-ward.) (5198)

And sometimes there are passages in which the motion of the characters is seen against a background that seems to fly by:

> Tree after tree, with what mad haste
> They rush past us as we go,
> See the boulders bending low,
> And the rocks of long-nosed sort
> How they snore and how they snort.
> (3876–80) (P)

Even the beauty of woman has to be seen in motion to become an object of love. Chiron, the centaur who carried Helen of Troy on his back when she was a child, states (7399–405) that beauty which rests in itself is rigid, but that it becomes irresistible when it starts to move and overflow with joy and the love of life.

In the chapbook Faust has a strong desire to eliminate both time and space. He flies to the stars and, in thus overcoming the limitations of space, simultaneously overcomes time, at least for the non-duration of his flight. Goethe's hero, who is allowed a much longer life span, knows this desire too. But it does not have for him the urgency it has for the older Faustus, and although he wishes in vain that he could fly toward the sun, most of his desires are easily fulfilled.

What matters in Goethe's work is not the fulfillment of the hero's a-temporal and a-spacious wishes, but rather the creation of a poetic reality in which time and space have no realistic function except to represent dimensions of the mind and imagination. The overcoming of space is taken care of by the existence of a magic carpet which carries Faust and Mephistopheles wherever they want to go. In some instances there is even no carpet, and we suddenly find the strange couple in a place far away from that of the previous scenes. From the point of view of stage requirements, the overcoming of space is not really a problem. Goethe shows some of Shakespeare's sovereign disregard for changes in locale, and vastly enlarges on it. But he carries his delight in toying with space very far. When Faust leaves Greece, Helen's clothes transformed into a cloud carry him to the high Alps, and as he watches the disappearance of this cloud in the East, he sees simultaneously far in the Northwest the North Sea lapping the coast of the Netherlands. Neither Greece nor the Netherlands are literally named in this scene, but they are clearly suggested. As Mephistopheles joins Faust—using seven league boots—they step down in no time to the foothills where the battle of Act IV will take place.

Time is as easily overcome on stage as place, and Goethe uses every possible device at his disposal to indicate the timelessness of the events of Faust's life. We are dealing here, however, with a more complex problem. On the one hand, Faust, though at first rejuvenated, is subject to the laws of maturing and aging. We are never told

his age nor how much time he spends in this action or that, until
we learn, in Act V, that he is one hundred years old and that time,
even for him, will "stand still." On the other hand, within the span
of his long life, time operates in interesting ways to accomplish
mythical events. Thus Helen of Troy, coming back to Greece after
the Trojan War, walks immediately into Faust's medieval castle.
She and her maidens travel from Sparta to the northern Peloponne-
sus in the time span of a few minutes, yet centuries pass of which
we are unaware. Similarly, her son grows from childhood to adult-
hood within moments—and with his growth several further historical
centuries are disposed of. Another reversal of time takes place in the
case of Homunculus; having destroyed his vial at the feet of Galatea,
he will start life at the beginning of time.

Even more complex is the treatment of causation and motivation.
Cause-effect relationships in this mythical world are as loosely
handled as psychological motivation. Sometimes they are supplied,
but just as often as not the perplexed reader or listener asks in vain
why certain events occur. We are never told why Faust should appear at the Emperor's court, or why Menelaos, although not coming
on stage, should twice be heard. The reader is expected to take at
face value so many astonishing things—such as spirits, monsters, and
witches—that the absence of causality becomes as acceptable as the
fluidity of time and space. Where causality is needed for the understanding of the meaning, however, Goethe provides it. In the purely
human realm of Gretchen, causality is strictly adhered to, as it is
again in the fifth act, in the story of Philemon and Baucis.

Psychological motivation is a somewhat different problem because
it so greatly affects the believability of the hero. Goethe offers us a
good deal of it, as when Faust despairs of the insufficiency of scholarship. But even here much of the motivation for action or suffering
goes beyond directly determinable psychological sources. We must
keep in mind that the work is more world oriented than mind oriented, and that its myths depict the external world rather than the
human mind. Its purpose is often not to explore the depth of Faust's
mind, but to place him in such a relation to the given world that he

may view it without despair. The moments in Faust's life when his subconscious *is* suddenly revealed therefore stand out. Such moments occur with his reawakened childhood memory during Easter night, with the shudder that seizes him when Mephistopheles mentions the Mothers, with his sudden vision of Gretchen and the red band around her neck while he is dancing with a witch. Mostly, however, Goethe does not conceive Faust as a man burdened by memories.

Often psychological motivation is less significant than symbolic value. Faust's claustrophobic reaction in his study is a good example of the dual interpretation required in such scenes. While he certainly feels hemmed in and almost strangled by his environment, his response is also intended to convey to us a statement about the limitations of scholarship in general. Similarly, at the beginning of Act IV, when we find him in the Alps, we must be aware that the vastness of the view not only corresponds to Faust's desire for large views —in contrast to his former life in his study—but is at the same time a symbolic image of the growth of his mind. There are other scenes requiring dual interpretation. The beginning of Part II with its health-restoring magic is such a moment. After a night's sleep Faust's guilt feelings disappear. This is the naked psychological fact. But what we see on stage are the songs and actions of spirits whose words dispel the guilt feelings. The magic of the Witches' Kitchen with its awakening of sexual desires is likewise a psychological moment transformed into a symbolic scene. Even Faust's dreams are art works rather than memories. As a revelation of his subconscious they are, I believe, useless because they are too obvious, too complete, too formed into consistent images and stories. They resemble daydreams in which the mind *creates* a story rather than chaotic night dreams, rising from the subconscious.

As was noted earlier, man's inner drives manifest themselves in the poem as demonic powers. Goethe follows here the method of ancient myth, one of whose characteristic features it is to transform human forces into mythological characters and stories. Though the reader should recognize Goethe's intention to externalize internal events, he should not interpret these mythological features necessarily as allegories of the mind. Sometimes they represent Faust's own dark forces, but more often they are representations of universal energies surpassing the individual's narrow range.

IRONY AND SATIRE

If myth is the warp of the poem, irony is its woof. Faust's higher and lower soul—his spiritual striving, which is, for better or worse, coupled with his sensuous desires—clearly calls for a dualistic treatment. Mephistopheles is therefore provided to serve as the representative of man's physical nature, of the beast in man. In addition he makes a witty, ironic, cynical companion. The Lord likes him because he is a rogue. In contrast to Faust's humorlessness—a smiling Faust being completely unthinkable—the devil provides the play with laughter. Just as man on earth—like it or not—is tied to his body, so Faust is bound to his laughing, irreverent companion.

This is a blessing from a reader's or spectator's point of view. Without it, nothing would be more tedious than Faust's eternal yearning for idealistic solutions he never finds. But for every one of them Mephistopheles supplies the right ironic puncture. He deflates Faust as often as Faust begins to soar; and while this hurts the hero's finer feelings, he cannot escape the realization that Mephistopheles is partly right. So we have the alternately painful and ridiculous spectacle of a man whose appealing romantic yearnings are constantly dissolved in his companion's acid remarks. Mephistopheles's down to earth realism is actually closer to our own thinking than the ever-deluded dreams of Faust. The devil calls things by their true name (3294–95), exposing the real motives behind the sham actions. No weakness or frailty escapes him, and he thus becomes, paradoxically, the only truly honest character in the work. Since he is not subjected to emotions, he can laugh where others suffer. But even his laughter is not offensive, because of its fundamental honesty and truth. Nothing and no one in the entire poem, including Helen of Troy, escapes being commented on mockingly by Mephistopheles, and often by other characters. Except for the angels, who have only one viewpoint, and Mephistopheles, who maintains the opposite point of view, no character in the play stands on solid ground. The function of the devil is precisely to prevent anyone's doing so. There is doubt, mockery, foul play in every phase of the work as soon as Mephistopheles appears on the stage.

Each time Faust realizes the truth of Mephistopheles' irony he gets angry. The closer the devil's irony hits home, the angrier he becomes. For him the ironic mode of his companion is disgusting and, although true, ultimately unacceptable. There is not a single passage in the whole work where Faust returns irony with irony. He can order the devil around, but he cannot rise above him to the point where the ironic stance would pass from Mephistopheles to himself. In this respect the protagonist never grows, and the function of the two characters and their interrelationship remains the same throughout the work.

Other characters in the work are mocked at with the same intent of revealing their weaknesses. The student who later appears as Baccalaureus is a prime victim of Mephistopheles' deflating irony. The philosopher Anaxagoras in the Classical Walpurgisnight, whose "volcanistic" theory of the origin of life Goethe despised, is made ridiculous when he sees the moon coming down to destroy the earth, an event on which Thales drily comments:

> What things the good man saw and heard:
> Myself I know not what occurred.
> Nor of such feelings was aware.
> Let us confess, there's madness in the air:
> Yet Luna yonder seems to hold
> Her course as calmly as of old.
>
> (7930–35)

At times, particularly in Part II, Goethe's irony turns even against the devil. We see him made fun of in the Classical Walpurgisnight by the ancient monsters who are older and wiser than he. At the end of the play we see him lose his bet, in a particularly ludicrous scene. The play thus takes back much of Faust's own seriousness through the author's ironic mode. Even the Lord in the Prologue in Heaven is spoken of mockingly by the devil.

The irony so pervasively present in the play is not its only deflating device. Satire—not frequently used by Goethe—is just as prevalent. From Faust's serious vows of eternal love for Margaret to the events at the Emperor's court, there stretches a line of satire which could hardly be more devastating to human institutions and beliefs. The court scenes in which the devil is allowed full play are an especially grand occasion for biting satire. Nor does the scope of Goethe's satire stop there. It hits the Christian religion and its institutions just as hard as the worldly institutions.

> The church with a capacious maw is blest:
> Whole countries she has stowed away,
> Yet had no surfeit to this day;
> The church alone, dear ladies, can digest
> Ill-gotten goods with real zest.
>
> (2836–40)

Thus a duality of viewpoint is always present and we would be quite wrong to take sides. The rhythm of the play demands an alternation of high aspirations and devilish irony, each negating the other. Faust is not upbraided by a moralist, but laughed at by a wit whose realistic outlook on human nature is sharper and more penetrating than his own. Thus the danger of moralism is avoided without the loss of moral judgments. The reader must realize, however, that there exists a difference between a serious censure of evil deeds and the ironic posture that Mephistopheles takes. The devil cannot possibly wish to improve Faust's moral position. So, though the devil's irony lays bare Faust's weaknesses, these weaknesses are not condemned either by him or by the author. The serious reader may condemn them; the play does not. Irony thus adds a dimension to the dialectics of good and evil: It does not pass judgment, but holds a pointing finger up and smiles.

ELEMENTS OF FORM

THE DRAMATIC DIALOGUE

Faust is not a drama in the ordinary sense and its plot does not obey obvious dramatic rules. What we generally consider essential to dramatic plot, namely, an interaction among a few human beings whose essential characteristics are thus revealed, is conspicuously absent. Instead, Faust's life unfolds in many apparently disconnected scenes, giving us glimpses of his responses in selected situations. The play is un-Aristotelian and unclassical in the sense that it defies the unities of time, place, and action. It is also doubtful whether any catharsis takes place either in the main character or in the audience, nor can it be said with conviction that the play moves an audience to pity and fear.

More fundamental still is the question whether *Faust* is a stage play at all. Both parts have been and are being presented both in Germany and other countries; the first part, when well produced, can be effective. That the work as a whole cannot be played without cutting appears obvious from its sheer size. But this is not the foremost objection a director might have. In addition to its disregard of time and place, *Faust* calls for difficult stage effects. Clouds must form, fire must be produced and extinguished, sunlight must be reflected in a waterfall and produce a rainbow, spirits must speak or sing invisibly, Homunculus must light up in a test tube. The plot obviously embraces much more than human emotions. And while all of this can be staged in a modern theatre, the question remains whether it is effective and whether it can hold an audience's attention.

What can be said without hesitation is that the Faust story, as Goethe conceives it, belongs to dialogue rather than to narrative. Although it presents a man's life from his youth to his grave and would thus seem equally suited for an epic or a novel, this particular man and this particular plot would make little sense if told by the narrative medium. Faust the character is engaged in a lifelong dialogue, partly with the devil, partly with a woman, partly with nature or the world at large, partly with human institutions or mythical situations. Never at peace with himself or the world, he finds himself in a situation of conflict: Faust has to conquer or be conquered, to act and react. As he suffers from the existence of his two souls, of the conflict between mind and body, good and evil, aspirations and disappointments, so his relation to the world falls into dialectical patterns. Nothing less than a dialogue could have expressed this experience of strife, of acceptance and rejection, of ambition and failure.

THE EPISODIC STRUCTURE

The play proceeds in a large number of scenes chosen by the author to provide his hero with a variety of encounters. Most of them have brief titles. They are not logically connected, but put together in clusters, centering each on one major event. Even in Part II, which Goethe divided into acts, the acts are split into individual scenes, most of them carrying titles, like the scenes in Part I. We may think of them as tableaux, if we keep in mind that each is a tableau in motion, not a still life.

The scenes vary greatly in length and in the number of characters appearing in them. When Faust arrives at the Emperor's court, we have a fairly long and crowded scene, since the splendor of the court must be seen and felt if the audience is to understand its meaning in the play. More often the scenes are short, expressing an important moment in a few lines. The shortest is that entitled "Night. Open Plain," in which Faust and Mephistopheles ride past a tombstone at night. They appear like restless ghosts, and the few prose lines spoken in alternation enhance the impression of ghosts swishing by.

In classical tragedies time tends to stand still for the short period of the play. The culminating moment of a man's life is singled out and made, as it were, eternal. Goethe handles Faust's life in exactly the opposite way. Selecting a variety of moments from Faust's long life, he stresses the flow of time by presenting them as episodes. The relentless flow of life is captured in the brevity and rapid sequence of dramatic scenes.

That these scenes are not arbitrarily linked, but follow each other with a complete logic of the imagination is particularly evident in the Gretchen story. Here the events, which must cover approximately one year, build one on the other with poignant inner necessity, each one representing an essential moment in the evolution of the tragedy. Thus the scene "At the Well" (3544–86) introduces two girls chatting lightly about the pregnancy of a third girl, while Gretchen is filled with pity. In the next scene (3588–619) she prays to the Mother of God to help her in her own shame. And in the subsequent scene, "Night," her brother accuses her of being a whore, and makes her shame known to everyone. The reader is stunned by the laconic brevity with which the highlights of Margaret's life are singled out. The same may be said of the articulation of scenes throughout the work: Any change in their order would blur the inner logic of their sequence.

THE "REALMS" OF THE PLAY

Within the basic episodic structure, three main layers of material may be discerned.

Certain events will be seen to make best sense when simply considered as the inheritance of the old puppet play. The figure of the Lord at the beginning and of hell's mouth at the end are to be regarded in that light. The Lord of the Prologue in Heaven, who is almost comical, cannot be identified with the world-soul that inspires all life. He stems from the old puppet play and need not be over-interpreted. The signing of the pact with a drop of blood falls into the same category. Most of the characters, too, introduce themselves with a few self-explanatory lines such as occur frequently in puppet plays. Even Faust and Margaret when they first appear tell the audience who they are.

Certain other aspects of the play derive from Goethe's effort to give Faust an aura of authenticity as a Renaissance man.[9] Many scenes, in Faust's "Gothic" study[10] as well as at the Emperor's court, belong clearly to that period; so does the nature of the play's magic, which on its literal level closely follows sixteenth-century practices. On the other hand, Goethe realized that the archaic language of the Faust book could not serve his purposes, since he did not basically intend to describe a historical hero, but a man contemporary to his own age. Faust's feelings, like his search for enlightenment and peace of mind, clearly belong to Goethe's own times, and his language reflects this. We are therefore faced with a man whose outer trappings are of the sixteenth century, but whose inner makeup— emotions, thoughts, speech—belongs to the early nineteenth century. To call this a historical play, as dealing with the period in which the story is laid, is of course wrong. Actually, the sixteenth century must be regarded as a symbolic setting, representing a time after the Middle Ages when all the human options were again open. The sixteenth-century setting is thus a frame, and the tension between it and the modern outlook remains a fascinating feature of Goethe's *Faust*.

Still other layers and realms exist in the play, often as the ambience of a particular personage. Perhaps the foremost example is the Catholic world in which Gretchen lives, thinks, and dies. She judges both Faust and Mephistopheles from her own religious point of view, impervious to Faust's pantheistic enthusiasm, and Faust never tries to dispel her belief. Similarly, Faust's apprentice Wagner has an ambience suggesting the "age of enlightenment" against which Goethe and his young friends had strongly rebelled. In Wagner, in fact, as in Faust himself, two historical elements are joined. As befits a man of the sixteenth century, Wagner is learning from Faust, among other things, to be an alchemist. But in Part I he is portrayed as a bookish and rationalistic pedant, the kind of "enlightened" professor of whose type Goethe knew only too many specimens.

The mythological layerings vary greatly. Where Mephistopheles is the center, we are in a Nordic realm of witches and witchcraft. Where Homunculus takes over we are in a realm of ancient Mediterranean life-giving deities and monsters. Helen belongs to two mythological periods, that of Homeric times as well as that of Euripides' *The Trojan Women,* from which Goethe adopted the chorus of women. Another vast realm is that of neo-Platonic demonology and angelology; Homunculus himself stems from this realm, and so do the angels. In a paradoxical way we might say that such variety provides one of the unifying bonds of the work.

TREATMENT OF CHARACTERS

Faust is crowded with characters, important as well as minor "mythological" and human individuals or types. Their great number is an indication of Faust's movement through many realms of life. Mythological characters, particularly, abound: spirits, monsters, demons, witches. Some of these Faust finds it hard to come to terms with. Others he barely notices or ignores, especially those who make him sleep or dream. Some hover on the verge of abstraction and allegory, like the Earth-Spirit at the beginning and Care at the end of the play. Others are more fully realized, like Mephistopheles, Homunculus, Euphorion. All of them are handled in the work with great freedom. Many seem to have an entirely independent existence, their relationship to Faust appearing to be accidental, indifferent, and neutral. Some are "good," for example, Ariel and his friends; others are evil and in the direct service of the devil, for example, the three powerful helpers. But they all have one common function essential to their role in the work—they affect Faust's life. Whether he accepts, rejects, or ignores them, they exist only in relation to him. We may call them features of the subconscious or agents of destiny—they are the benevolent or malignant forces in Faust's pilgrimage.

Among the lesser characters some have considerable importance.

For instance, the three young boys, Homunculus, the Boy-Chario-teer, and Euphorion, are incipient Faust figures. All of them have distinct personalities in addition to their allegorical status. This is even true for Homunculus, who has no body, only intelligence and intuition. Lovable and everybody's darling, he has a commanding presence and is able to order Mephistopheles around as only Faust can do. As much may be said of the Boy-Charioteer and Euphorion: The humanity of these unearthly creatures outshines their lack of "reality." They bring into the strange world of the aging Faust the necessary youthfulness which can give new impetus to the hero's endeavors. They also bring a new innocence that makes the reader aware of possibilities for life after Faust's death. On the human level, possibly, they represent the "real" son Faust never had.

Another character who is both symbolical and "real" is the guardian Lynceus.[11] He is the first to see Helen coming and forgets his duty at the sight of her beauty. In a manner differing from that of the boys he, too, is a Faust figure. He is stung to the quick by Helen's beauty because, being like Faust a "visual" type, visual impressions move him deeply. The same is true for his second appearance, in Act V, where he guards Faust's palace. As he watches the fire that destroys the little hut of the old couple, the sight causes him pain as great as he felt on Helen's approach. He has a free and open view of the land Faust so ardently desires, but each time he "sees," something—good or bad—disturbs the clear, disinterested vision. For he, too, is human and hence vulnerable.

Only few major figures have a prolonged and lasting relationship with Faust. Characteristically, the devil is the only permanent companion of the hero who, although having a *famulus,* never had a friend. Moreover, two women, one real and one mythological, are of major importance. From a merely formal point of view, these characters have the same function as the minor characters discussed earlier: They are both individuals and symbols and their relationship to Faust is simultaneously mutually effective and highly symbolic.

A word needs to be said about Faust's own character. Although his impulses cannot be called evil, he unwittingly stumbles into situations which cause him to harm other human beings. He is driven rather than driving, conquered rather than conquering, a responder rather than an agent. In everything, including his love for Margaret, he remains a self-centered monomaniac, obsessively bent on finding answers to his disturbing questions about the meaning of life. His relations to others are colored by his personality and do not represent an honest attempt to understand the other person, or to truly act in his own behalf. There is also no trace of humility in him, but rather the hubris of a man who believes that answers to his questions are within reach. His redeeming features are the vastness of his mind and the degree of self-knowledge which allows him to anticipate the traps which he builds for himself. He is always simultaneously engaged by an action and yet apart from it through his insight into its futility. What he knows and what he knows he does not know, create the dialectics of his mind and spur him on to new and different experiences. From a symbolistic point of view he represents Life in the widest sense.

METERS AND RHYMES

An engaging aspect of the work is the poet's virtuosity with meters and rhymes. Goethe adapted to the language all the meters used in the Western world from antiquity on: hexameters, blank verse, Alexandrines, the short lines of medieval Latin hymns, the trimeter of Greek drama, and the irregular *Knittelvers* of the German sixteenth century. He wrote popular ballad meters as well as anacreontics. Above all he liked the hymnic stanza of Pindar, and in developing it he created his own original form of free verse.

Knittelvers

This is a rather rough meter, used by the German artisans of the sixteenth century. Despite elaborate rules it is ponderous rather than elegant. Apart from the Margaret scenes, Goethe uses it mainly to characterize Faust in his Gothic environment. It conveys in its stiffness and lack of even flow the uneasiness of Faust the scholar. Faust's very first words are written in it.

> I now have studied Philosophy,
> And Law and Medicine to boot,
> And (sad to tell) Theology,
> From end to end in Wisdom's hot pursuit.
>
> (354–57)

When in Part II Faust is carried back in a trance to his old dusty room, which has grown gloomier over the years, Mephistopheles takes up the meter again in speaking with the various characters he meets there.

Knittelvers had some distinct advantages for Goethe. For one thing, the irregular number of unaccented syllables and the changing stress on the first or second syllable of each line allow this meter to be assimilated to free verse, in which the poet had always permitted himself a great amount of freedom. Since the reader does not expect a definite number of syllables or a clearly defined stress, he is not put off by the frequent insertion of longer or shorter lines. When the Earth-Spirit prepares his appearance, for instance, Faust's meter changes to free verse:

> Clouds gather over me—
> The moon conceals its light—
> The lamp has vanished!
> Mists rise!—Red lightnings dart and flash
> About my head—Down from
> The vaulted roof cold horror blows
> And seizes me!
> Spirit implored, I feel you hovering near.
> Reveal yourself!
>
> (468–77) (P)

As the lines become shorter and more irregular, the exitement that precedes the actual appearance of the spirit is clearly felt. But as soon as the Earth-Spirit appears, both he and Faust fall back into *Knittelvers*, that is, from a hymnic invocation to colloquialism.

A further advantage of this meter was its flexibility. If its unstressed syllables are limited to one, it can be made into smooth iambics, as in some of the Gothic scenes. With the addition of an extra iamb, it can become blank verse—of which, in memory of his beloved Shakespeare, Goethe was particularly fond. Most conversations between Faust and Mephistopheles are written in a meter of four, five or sometimes six, iambs, developed from the *Knittelvers.* It is the prevailing meter of the dramatic dialogue.

The Medieval Hymnic Meter

I use the term *medieval* to distinguish these hymns from the Pindaric hymns of Goethe's early poetry. But their medieval quality is Goethe's own invention. He does not follow the medieval rhythmic pattern that is exemplified in the *Dies Irae* of the Cathedral scene. This hymn has a line of four stresses, whereas Goethe's own hymns have only two. It remains true, nevertheless, that his intention was to produce a medieval impression.

These religious hymns occur in the early scene of the Easter night, and then again at the very end of Part II, where they are patterned after the early scenes. Their distinctive characteristic is the presence of two unstressed syllables after each main stress. The German language needs such a meter for the special reason that adjectives and participles very often end in two unstressed syllables. Goethe manipulated his lines in such a way as to place both present and past participles in their conjugated forms (ending in two unstressed syllables) at the end of the lines, rhyming not only two, but often four or five of these participial adjectives and thus creating a solemnity which he carefully reserved for religious purposes.

> *Tätig ihn Preisenden,*
> *Liebe Beweisenden,*
> *Brüderlich Speisenden,*
> *Predigend Reisenden*
> (801–804)[12]

The famous last stanza of the entire work follows this pattern, using adjectives instead of participles, but clearly reminding the reader of the hymn that praised the resurrection of Christ (737 ff). As Christ has arisen, so Faust is carried upward.

In a slightly simplified form, the same meter, although without the complex rhyme scheme, is used for the songs of the spirits

(1447–1505 and others). Despite the fact that these spirits here obey Mephistopheles' order, they are not in any way evil spirits. They are the "neutral" spirits which occur throughout Renaissance literature and are considered to be distant relatives of the angels. The use of the hymnic meter is in itself a clue to Goethe's view of their nature.

Songs and Ballads

This is a vast field. Almost everyone, with the exception of Faust, sings at one time or another. Gretchen sings the ballad "The King of Thule" which, although original with Goethe, is shaped as a folk ballad. Toward the end of Part I, in her state of insanity, she sings folk songs after the manner of Ophelia in *Hamlet*. The devil sings to lure her brother out of the house; students sing drinking songs, etc. In Part II the songs often have more solemnity, as in the songs of Lynceus, the guardsman. But at the Emperor's court during the Mardi Gras festivities light-hearted songs appear in great numbers. All of these songs are written to be sung. Their presence in the work emphasizes the fact that Goethe at times thought that *Faust* should be made into an opera.

The Classical Meters

The most notable classical meter in the poem is the trimeter of the ancient tragedies, which is always unrhymed, and which, in *Faust,* contrasts vividly with the Alexandrines used at the Emperor's court in imitation of Racine's rhymed couplets. The trimeters in *Faust* are mainly reserved for Helen of Troy. Her chorus uses a more strophic stanza with a distinct ancient flavor (see for example, 9482–505). In contrast to the chorus, Faust's speeches and Lynceus' songs in the same act have rhymes, and Helen considers it a symbol of her new union with Faust that she learns to speak in rhymes.

In general, Goethe attributed considerable expressive value to both meter and rhyme. They are handled throughout with great care and deliberation. Very often we can read Goethe's true intention from the meter or rhyme scheme and we must certainly never disregard it. It is an indicator of relationships and a clear hint at meanings.

LANGUAGE

Goethe's expressive use of meters and rhymes is matched by an expressive use of idiomatic language. Each character has his own vocabulary. The devil enjoys the German equivalent of four-letter words; Gretchen speaks in a simple, somewhat pastoral vein; Faust's tone is always elevated. In the scenes in which many characters are present, each distinguishes himself by his diction.

One example of this is in the dialogue between Margaret and Faust when she asks him directly: "Do you believe in God?" (3426). Her next, equally simple and direct question: "Then you do not believe?" (3430), is answered by Faust in his typical high-flown tone:

> My answer, dear one, do not misconceive!
> Who can name
> Him, or proclaim:
> I believe in Him?
> Who is so cold
> As to make bold
> To say: I do not believe in Him?
> The all-embracing,
> The all-sustaining,
> Does He not hold and sustain
> You, me, Himself?
>
> (3431–40)   (P)

At the end of that scene Mephistopheles enters with words characteristic of his speech: "The little monkey's gone?" (3521).

Equally important is the presence of distinct rhetorical levels of style: Mephistopheles's low style is set off against Faust's high-flown language. Faust himself considers his lyrical voice to be his true voice. But it is always contrasted to the cold, often vulgar, cynical voice of Mephistopheles, which deflates and ridicules it. Thus a truly dramatic contrast exists between a lyrical and an ironic language, each typifying the character who speaks it and both together expressing the polarity of outlook on which the drama of the work depends. Faust's lyrical voice is an essential part of the dramatic dialogue.

To see how this counterpoint functions, we may turn to the famous scene, "Forest and Cavern." There Mephistopheles has just praised his office as pander when Faust realizes the misery he is about to prepare for his beloved Gretchen. He then compares himself with the roaring waterfall that yearns for the abyss, while the beloved lives nearby on a small Alpine meadow in great peace. But for him it is not enough to tear down rocks in his violent course, he must also undermine her world. This is a poetic image of great power, but it is typically a poetic image rather than a moral response even at this moment when, shortly before seducing Gretchen, Faust realizes the enormity of the harm he will do to her. Far from becoming dramatic, he becomes lyrical. His is essentially an aesthetic sensibility which evades moral categories and indulges instead in poetic language and imagery.

Goethe's attention to language in the poem extends also to sound; alliterations, assonances, poetic repetitions and echoes abound. He enjoys inventing words the sound of which is a comic imitation of what is happening on the stage. Thus the word *Schneckeschnicke-schnack* (4257) imitates the Orchestra in the Walpurgisnight Dream, more specfically the bagpipe. Then, too, the griffins in Part II prove "etymologically" to what realm of life they wish to belong, the name being derived from German *greifen,* "to grab" (7093–98).

Puns are another comic device. Since their effectiveness is lost in translation, only one example will be mentioned. When the Emperor signs the paper money it is quickly multiplied by what are ironically called "magicians," perhaps better "Jacks-of-all-trades." The German terms for "multiply" and "Jack-of-all-trades" both contain the word "thousand" although the terms themselves are in no way related. Goethe's verse here (*Durch Tausendkünstler schnell vertausendfacht*) by its clever repetition of *tausend,* suggests the Emperor turning out bills by the thousands—instant currency derived from a play on words!

❧ V ❧

THE PLOT

THE STRUCTURE OF THE UNIVERSE

Faust is the last of a long series of European poems which present poetically both the universe as a whole and the earth's relationship to it. True, only a few lines are devoted to the world-view in Faust; most of the work takes place, often painfully, on earth and in the life of an earthly hero. We are frequently reminded, however, mainly by mention of the symbolic sun, of the structure of the whole, in which Faust's life is embedded.

The Prologue in Heaven, from which we learn something of the poem's world-view, is divided into two distinct parts: Three stanzas, sung by the archangels at the beginning in praise of the creation, give us the most complete picture of the cosmos we will ever receive; and a dialogue follows between the Lord and Mephistopheles which sets the stage for the rest of the action.

The rhythmic scheme of the angelic song is solemn. It has four iambic feet in each line, to which an unaccented half-foot is added with complete regularity at the end of alternating lines.

$$\smile \; / \;\; \smile \; / \;\; \smile \; / \;\; \smile \; / \;\; \smile$$
$$\smile \; / \;\; \smile \; / \;\; \smile \; / \;\; \smile \; /$$

Each of its three stanzas has eight lines. The rhyme scheme (*ab ab cd cd*) follows from the rhythmic arrangement, inasmuch as the alternating accented and the alternating unaccented syllables rhyme. In his few contemplative moments during the play (for example, his Bible translation, 1178–85 and 1194–201) Faust follows the same rhythmic pattern. As soon as Mephistopheles starts to speak, the pattern changes to five accented syllables. For a while his rhymes tend to follow the angels' alternating ones, but soon change to less rigorous patterns. Thus the shift of rhyme scheme marks a change from song to spoken word. It also marks the difference between the perfection of the angels and the casualness of Mephistopheles.

In the angelic stanzas we hear about the harmony of the spheres and the incomprehensible but grand course of the sun and the planets. We are told that the earth in its eternal rotation is the place of light and darkness and of a perpetual and seemingly sense-less motion of storms, water, and clouds. To this violent vision of the earth the angels understandably prefer the "gentle movement of God's day." Throughout the poem we will be confronted with the violent motion of storms, water, and clouds, and we will over and over again be reminded of the alternation of day and night. Within the harmony of the spheres, the earth remains the unharmonious spot to which man is confined.

At the end of the work Faust's immortal part is carried upward, and we hope that the angelic vision of harmony will now be given to him. But not a word is said of this possibility. The immortal part of Faust is still very closely linked to his life on earth. Though his rise may gradually free him from this, it will not happen before the end. Not even so much as the incomprehensible spectacle of the planetary motions is repeated.

The rest of the Prologue as well as the entire play is concerned with one man's life on earth. Never again are we reminded of uni-versal harmony. The sun, mentioned throughout as the symbol of understanding, will be the only connecting link between the first three stanzas and Faust's dark life.

While we are still in the presence of the Lord and the angels, Faust's life is predetermined. As in the Book of Job, the Lord points out His trusted servant to the "Spirit of Negation," Mephistopheles, to prove His complete trust in the human being whom He has selected for temptation. Unlike the Book of Job, however, Meph-istopheles suggests a wager regarding Faust, very sure that he will win it. To parry this suggestion formally would be beneath the dignity of the Lord, but it is clear from His words that, as in Job, He will allow Mephistopheles to lead Faust astray "if he can do it" and that He, too, expects to win. Implicit in everything He says is the calm confidence that, no matter what Mephistopheles may try to do, the good man will find himself through his errors. Since the Lord, being the Lord, must, in some sense, win the wager, it is clear that Faust will in the end be "saved"—whatever that may prove to mean.

We learn very little in the Prologue about the Lord, who is not portrayed as the Creator of everything living. By contrast much is stated about the nature of Mephistopheles. He is not a fallen angel; he is free to roam the earth; he finds man's life pitiful and does not understand man's effort to rise from the dust to which he will fall back anyway. He understands Faust least of all because, up to now, he has had no hold on him. We realize that this will change in the future, for Mephistopheles has, we know, another side, which endears him immediately to the Lord and also to the reader: he is a rogue. As such he will not permit Faust to settle down, but instead will spur him on to continued activity. This, at least, is the devil's function as seen from the viewpoint of the Lord.

Despite the light tone of the dialogue, the Lord's words have to be taken seriously. Many of them are repeated in the very last scene, thus indicating their importance. At the moment they are first spoken they set the stage for the future association between a man who walks in darkness and who errs and a devil who tries to increase his errors, but who, as the Prologue makes very clear, will not succeed. Exit at this point the Lord, who has fulfilled his task.

Faust, the Scholar and His Ironic Counterparts

When we see Faust for the first time in his Gothic room, with its small, darkened windows, its chemical retorts and dusty books, he has been a teacher for ten years. He has learned all there is to learn at a sixteenth-century university and he realizes that this knowledge has neither given him much satisfaction nor brought him wealth. In his general discontent he has turned to magic, from which he expects answers to his gnawing questions; he wants to find —in contrast to the "empty words" science has given him—"what holds the world in its essence together." This is a desire typical of scholarship in the late sixteenth century. It amounts to a pansophic faith which may give to a man who uses magic correctly and in a religious spirit intuitive insight into the ultimate harmony the angels have praised.

But already in Faust's first monologue there are strange contradictions. His desire, as he describes it, does not really seem to be concerned with the essence of the world, but rather with its outward appearance. He longs to be on the mountains, or in moonlit meadows, and he contrasts his dusty and musty study with life in "living nature." More and more it becomes clear that what Faust calls magic is to be for us a poetic expression of a new approach to nature. We learn gradually that we are not dealing with an aging sixteenth-century *alchemist,* but rather with a youthful eighteenth-century *enthusiast* who has been called on, by Rousseau as well as by his own inclination, to "return to nature." But this eighteenth-century desire is expressed in terms of the sixteenth century: Faust feels "the spirits of nature hovering around him." For a moment, looking at the magic sign of the macrocosm, he thinks with delight that his mind's eye can see "creative nature" itself. A symbolic sign is not reality, however, and Faust quickly realizes his inability to conjure up what is too vast for his understanding—just as the universe was too vast for the understanding of the angels. Imitating the sequence of the angels' song, he turns therefore from the universe to the Spirit of the Earth, whom he invokes only to be told that he does not understand him.

This entire first scene gives the reader a reliable portrait of the hero. He is impatient, restless, given to hyperbole both in happiness and despair, emotional and often quite irrational, but possessing great power of mind and speech, and the strength of a vivid imagination. He is not quite creative enough to be a poet, and the work can therefore not be classified as the tragedy of an artist. On the other hand, he has an observant and searching mind which, while insufficient to make him a poet, prevents him from being satisfied with scholarship. He wholeheartedly rejects all that he has devoted his life to, including even his home. His great previous effort to acquire knowledge and preserve his home has now no conceivable value for him. As the play unfolds we will see that it is not just this particular knowledge or home that he rejects; everything he gains or acquires will likewise turn to nothing in his hands. He is by nature, for better or worse, a dissatisfied person to whom nothing will ever suffice. That this is a negative characteristic is more readily seen than that it is also a positive one. For a moment we may think that Mephistopheles' comparison, in the Prologue, likening man to a cicada that alternately flies and falls down, is an extremely apt one, at least for this particular man. With his undefined longing for nature, yet real inability to hold on to the Earth-Spirit, he is in a pitiful situation, which seems entirely of his own making.

After his disastrous encounter with the Earth-Spirit, Faust is profoundly depressed and ready to commit suicide. That he does not carry out his intention is due to no new insight, but to a childhood memory evoked by the sudden sound of Easter bells. From the two viewpoints of psychology and the quest for knowledge this is one of Goethe's masterstrokes. In the monologue (762–83) which follows the Easter message that "Christ has arisen," these two viewpoints are clearly stated. In Faust's youth he had not, to be sure, possessed his present knowledge, but had instead owned a faith in the Christian message which was better than rational truth and which he has now lost. Miracles and the love of God found in him at that time a receptiveness which made it possible for him to create his own inner world (777). The knowledge of the world around him was of no concern, and no despair could mar the confidence in his inner universe. A memory of this state of mind and of the happiness of his youthful occupations arrests his hand as he is ready to drink poison, and he feels given "back to the earth." The renewed sense of past happiness strengthens him to carry on and prepares the way for his walk in the open fields. It is there that the devil first presents himself.

We may also attribute to this reawakened memory the circumstance that, on the same Easter Sunday evening, Faust sits down to translate the Bible. In view of his present life and his rejection of Christianity, however, it follows that the effort cannot succeed. Despite all his experience with words and their meanings, he ponders over a translation for the term "logos" at the beginning of the Gospel According to St. John, not realizing that the devil is already in his room and will make it impossible for him ever to return to scholarly pursuits. There is great suggestiveness, on Goethe's part, in setting the translation scene in the presence of Mephistopheles. From now on until Faust's death the Bible will be quoted only in a blasphemous way.

To emphasize the irrelevance of scholarship, Goethe ironically and satirically brings Wagner on stage, a caricature who is as happy in his book knowledge as his master is unhappy. He appears significantly, wearing his pedant's houserobe and nightcap, just after the Earth-Spirit has rejected Faust. He cares nothing for truth; his concern is only for the rhetoric a scholar needs to convince his contemporaries. But this, Faust retorts, is as empty as "the moaning autumn blast, which drives the dead leaves through the woodland ways" (556–57)—an image that Shelley was to remember and reapply. Taking up another metaphor, Faust suggests that the true source of life is not to be found in parchment but in man's heart. A hundred lines earlier he had longed for the "springs of life" (456–59) but, ironically, had been unable to find them in his heart. For Wagner, Faust's "other side," earthiness and sensuality do not exist and are no temptation. He honestly believes that he "knows much" and "would like to know all." When we meet him again in Part II, his studies have carried him in another direction. In imitation of Faust's alchemical endeavors, Wagner has managed to produce, without the help of natural procreation—again he is immune to sensuality —a little man in a test tube. The biting irony with which he is treated at this point finds its grotesque climax when Homunculus leaves him, as does Faust whose longed for presence in his house he has not even noticed.

While Wagner represents the inhuman extreme of scholarly pursuit, the student whom Mephistopheles strings along at the end of the Realm of Scholarship is an innocent and not very bright beginner. In this light and funny scene, the reverent student takes every word of the "master" seriously, while the audience, fully aware of the devil's work, laughs at his ridicule of precisely those topics that had caused Faust so much pain. When he advises the student about the practice of medicine, it is medicine with a difference.

> Next press her pulse (a safe advance!)
> And then with sly and fiery glance
> You'll catch her round her slender waist,
> To see how tightly she is laced.
>
> (2033–36)

Later, in Part II, we meet the same student, now Baccalaureus. He believes himself to be making fun of his former master, having grown considerably in the understanding of the nonsense of scholarship, but is in fact, once again, in the presence of a disguised Mephistopheles who exposes his posturings.

> BACHELOR:
> Experience? merely froth and bubble
> And with the mind not comparable:
> 'Tis scarcely worth the candle, you must own,
> To know the things which men have always known.
>
> (6758–61)

We thus witness three generations of scholars: the serious Faust, the pedant Wagner, and the empty-headed student.

Altogether, knowledge acquired through books, in whatever form it appears in the play, is either seriously or ironically rejected. The academic world is "dusty," "dead," "empty," "hollow." Mephistopheles appears in it only to lure Faust away, and in Faust's disgusted frame of mind this is an easy task. What Faust rejects in the world of learning is its narrowness of thought and experience, lack of inspiration, meager rewards and, perhaps most important, its meaningless use of words. Coupled with all this goes a rejection of abstract "reason" as arbiter of our actions in favor of emotionally and personally acquired experience. From now on and throughout Faust's long life he will follow his drives and desires rather than his rational judgment.

THE WAGER AND THE BET

The wager between the Lord and the devil has a fore-ordained outcome, for we are not dealing in *Faust* with an entirely anti-religious work. Goethe is a comprehensive iconoclast, but he does not deny the existence of a godhead. It is only that he keeps the terms of the wager vague. The Lord has confidence that a "good man in his dark drives is well aware of the right path." But is Faust a "good man"? And if so, is his goodness an ethical goodness? There is no doubt that he has "dark drives." Is he however "aware of the right path"? And again, is the right path a path of moral behavior?

The answers to these questions must derive from our study of the whole work. The Lord, we may assume, knows considerably more than He says about man's behavior on this earth, and His judgment —if He is the judge—must depend on criteria to which, in the Prologue, we are as yet given no clue.

The situation is completely different for Faust's bet with Mephistopheles. There is of course a pact as well, which Faust signs with his own blood, but this happens only after the conditions of the bet have been clearly defined. The pact is like the flourish at the end of a medieval manuscript—a written confirmation of something formulated beforehand in the words of the bet. The terms of this bet, in contrast to the terms of the wager in Heaven, are made extremely explicit.

The timing of the bet is also important. Faust has been rejected by the Earth-Spirit, has almost committed suicide, and has just lived through a scene in which he thought he could hold the devil captive, whereas the latter has cleverly escaped. This is the blackest moment of Faust's life and, in his disgust not only with book knowledge but with all experience, he curses everything that human beings consider of value.

My curse on all the powers that weave
Around the soul their guilded snare,
With arts that flatter and deceive
Confine it to this den of care;
Accursed be the self-esteem,
Wherewith the mind is fenced round:
Accurst the world of things that seem,
Whose shows bedazzle and confound;
Curse on our dreams, curse empty fancies,
The lure of place, of fame eterne,
And what as ownership entrances,
As plough and hind, as wife and bairn:
Accurst be Mammon, when with treasure
He urges us to valorous deed,
Or when upon the coach of leisure
He sets the cushions to our need!
Accurst the grape-vine's slumbrous potion,
Accurst the favours Love lets fall:
Accurst be Hope, and Faith's devotion,
And Patience curst above them all!

(1586–606)

Faust's sceptical mind has weighed the treasures of life and found them wanting. The best attractions the devil can offer after such a curse are certain to sound hollow. Therefore, in the full awareness of the relativity of joy, of the passing quality of happiness, of the comparative lack in value of every human achievement, Faust offers his bet: If you can deceive me with pleasure, he tells Mephistopheles, if I should ever wish a beautiful moment to last, then will I be ready to die. Goethe's hero, as opposed to Marlowe's, does not worry about a life hereafter and eternal punishment, but only expects to find out, with the devil's help, that life on earth has indeed nothing valuable or lasting to offer. With great consistency of character he looks ahead to new conquests that, like his former ones, will never satisfy. Does Faust need to learn from the devil something he has already found out? Obviously not. It is at this moment that Mephistopheles's symbolic role as Faust's "lower soul" becomes visible in the play.

There is one aspect of man's experience that Faust overlooks: When he condemned knowledge through books, he gave up a way of life. The first indication that there will be a significant change, if not in Faust's evaluation of experience, at least in the type of his experiences, is given in the Easter walk. After the Easter bells have called him away from suicide and back to the earth, he goes out into nature and meets human beings.[13] And although nature disappoints him, as everything else does, it is a first step beyond his study—and the devil, knowing this better than Faust, seizes the opportunity to present himself to Faust in the shape of a poodle. Expressive of this first step into life are the lines Faust speaks after signing the pact:

> My heart, now of the thirst of knowledge healed,
> Shall to no joy, no suffering be sealed:
> But in my inmost soul I'll feel and know
> Whatever man is doomed to here below!
> I'll scale the heights and plunge to the abyss,
> Heap on my breast man's woes and ecstasies!
> Till with the general self my single self shall blend,
> And in its ruin perish at the end!

(1768–75)

Unknown to Faust, in other words, is the fact that a man who is intent upon "entering into life" makes by necessity a pact with the "devil." As he shifts from intellectual to emotional experience, he takes a momentous step. To be sure, Faust has always had emotional reactions. His entire attitude toward knowledge attests to this. But all the experiences the rest of the play will present are new to him. Up to now, we suspect, he has neither loved a woman nor served at the court of the Emperor. In other words, his withdrawal into his study has shielded him from the experiences of life. He does not yet grasp that these experiences involve the basest as well as the finer instincts of man. He hardly knows what it means to hurt others and suffer from guilt feelings. He is scarcely even aware of his own sensibilities. He does not yet realize that what he is searching for is an active as opposed to a contemplative life. Though this new step will not change Faust's outlook on life, it will change, or perhaps better, fulfill, his personality. It will make him whole in the sense that it addresses itself to the whole man, his good and bad instincts, his emotions and his reason. Faust is rejuvenated, and the devil begins to play the part of his lower instincts.

The bet thus has a dimension unknown to Faust. He will of course continue to be restless and sceptical; no situation will ever deserve, in his judgment, a positive evaluation. The Lord knew this when he urged Mephistopheles to prevent Faust from "settling down" (340–43). In a decisive way Faust unknowingly follows the words of the wager between the Lord and the devil. What he cannot understand is that he is entering a kind of life very different from the one he had led in his study—a life exposed to the vicissitudes of existence, a life in which his "two souls" will come into play and in which their play will become a deadly serious issue.

It should be clearly understood that Faust's "higher" soul is quite divorced from "intellect." The latter persuaded him to find true knowledge in studies and is now fully rejected. What the higher soul really achieves is a kind of intuition, a felt truth, an immediate rather than a reasoned understanding; what Faust will allow himself to cherish in the future is the intuitive inspiration received through communion with Nature or beauty which opens up not so much a new realm of knowledge, as a new mode of understanding. To what extent even this type of understanding may be deceptive will become clear toward the end of the work.

MEPHISTOPHELES AND THE EARTH-SPIRIT

The Earth-Spirit, conjured up by Faust after he has contemplated the magic symbol of the macrocosm and found it overwhelming, is Goethe's own invention. He exists neither in the Faust legend nor in any books on magic. He appears to Faust in a moment of vision, introduces himself as the spirit of all activity from the cradle to the grave, and rejects Faust's claim to understand him. His nine short lines of self-description take up in part the angels' song about the earth: "In the tide of life, in the storms of deeds." In part, too, they express symbolically some of Faust's own actions and feelings: "I soar up and down, I weave back and forth." And in part they give a neo-Platonic explanation for all this seemingly meaningless activity by asserting that he thus weaves "on the rushing loom of time the godhead's living garment." The latter is a well-known neo-Platonic image which means that life on earth is only the outer appearance, but nonetheless a living appearance, of the world-soul.[14]

The Earth-Spirit thus represents all life on earth "from birth to the tomb" (504), not merely the physical side of man, but his actions, ambitions, insights. He is the symbol of everything, good or bad, physical or spiritual, great or mean, that Faust will ever experience. It is no wonder that, chained to the limiting experience of book learning, Faust cannot grasp the Earth-Spirit's full significance.

The Earth-Spirit, by withdrawing, leaves Faust shattered, dejected to the point of wanting to commit suicide. Yet he is not to be regarded as a negative influence. A little later in the work ("Forest and Cavern") Faust feels that he owes to the Earth-Spirit his present profound enjoyment of nature. In the same soliloquy he realizes that although he is beginning to understand the Earth-Spirit, he must in part pay for this understanding by being chained to Mephistopheles whom the Spirit gave him as a companion. Several other references here and there in the work seem to imply that Mephistopheles is somehow in the service of the Earth-Spirit.

This connection must not be taken too literally. Conceivably the earliest version of the work, in which there is no Prologue in Heaven, allowed for a direct relationship between the two spirits. But certainly, in the final version Mephistopheles comes of his own volition, and if anyone "sends" him it is the Lord. Taken in a somewhat less literal sense, on the other hand, the relationship between the two is close. Whereas in the hierarchy of spirits the Earth-Spirit is far above Mephistopheles and even above Faust, there can be no doubt that Mephistopheles inadvertently plays a part in the blessings that the Earth-Spirit bestows. Mephistopheles represents the "earthy" side of the Earth-Spirit. His strongest lure is sex—and we see him offering it freely in the Witches' Kitchen and the Walpurgisnight scenes. He will offer it again at the Emperor's court and on other occasions. Being tied to the earth, he cannot understand emotions that go beyond sex, but he does provide the earthly experience from which, for those under the tutelage of the Earth-Spirit, transcendent experiences arise.

The link between Mephistopheles and the Earth-Spirit is further made clear in the poem's images. The devil is "Lord of the Flies and the Mice," and wherever he enters his own realm, as in the Walpurgisnight, a low class of animals abounds.

> To-whit! To-whoo! it sounds away,
> Screech owl, plover, and the jay;
> Have all these stayed wide awake?
> Are those efts amid the brake?
> Long of haunch and thick of paunch!
> And the roots that wind and coil
> Snakelike out of stone and soil
> Knot the bonds of wondrous snares,
> Scare us, take us unawares;
> Out of tough and living gnarls
> Polyp arms reach out in snarls
> For the traveler's foot. Mice scurry
> Thousand-colored by drove and flurry
> Through the moss and through the heather!
> And the fireflies in ascent
> Densely swarm and swirl together
> Escort to bewilderment.
>
> (3889–905) (P)

We must recall, too, that Mephistopheles first appears as a poodle. His realm is the part of earth connected with lower forms of life, and in that area he serves the Earth-Spirit, as he does also, apparently, as custodian of gold and underground treasures. During the Walpurgisnight, he rejoices in the gold veins that glow underground. Through his interventions, paper money is minted at the Emperor's court. Riches are an essential part of his earthly-devilish realm—and he finds it disappointing that his victim has no interest in them. Equally disappointing to him is Faust's "regimen," as he calls Faust's spiritual search in the Prologue in Heaven. He finds his officiate quite unresponsive when they go to the students' drinking bout in Auerbach's Cellar.[15]

On all these grounds it is evident that Mephistopheles has, at a low level, some connection with the Earth-Spirit. It is also evident that such temptations as these cannot take very firm hold of a man like Faust. The devil's function is to put temptations before him so that he can reject them. This is not Mephistopheles's entire function, of course, but it is a consistent one throughout the work, and indicates his relationship to the Earth-Spirit.

Love and Sex

After the first fruitless stop at the student inn, Mephistopheles leads Faust to the Witches' Kitchen where he is perhaps not so much rejuvenated as sexually aroused. The scene is filled with erotic references and ends with the image of a woman whom Mephistopheles vaguely identifies as Helen of Troy. As soon as Faust steps on the stage in the next scene, he is attracted to Margaret and ready to seduce her. He is suddenly coarse, unscrupulous and, it seems, cured of his "higher aspirations." But this mood does not last. Even before he meets Gretchen in her neighbor's garden and learns to know her he has visited her room ("Evening"), asking the devil to leave him alone there; his "higher soul" begins to see her as a human being whom he respects and loves. As he realizes—and Faust is always conscious of his reactions—

> Erewhile my passion craved an instant bliss
> And now I float on dreams of happiness!
> (2722–23)

From this moment on the devil has his work cut out for him. As Faust hesitates and feels that he cannot and should not hurt Margaret, the devil takes on the role of tempter. The better Faust knows Margaret the more he would like to withdraw. But the devil waylays him and slyly urges him on to seduction.

Nowhere is the devil's role so clearly that of Faust's "lower soul" and nowhere does it so poignantly become plain that a man has indeed "two souls." Had Faust met a girl like Gretchen during his years in his study, he would have renounced her or perhaps never desired her. But, once out of his study and in the stream of life, this attitude is too simple. Fully aware of the meaning of his actions and their consequences Faust lies to Margaret, speaking as if his love were eternal. And yet, ironically, unbeknownst to him, it *has* an eternal aspect, which will be realized after death. Therefore, the two passages on the eternity of love (3061–66 and 3191–94) which seem to be false are more truly a paradox. Eternity is not of this earth, but it may be the design of the poem's heaven, where Faust's apprenticeship will once more begin with his encounter with Gretchen. And so, while he ruins her in life, his love remains eternal, as he had desperately wished it and deceitfully represented it to be.

The moral question is complicated by the fact that Goethe separates Margaret's morality from that of Faust. In contrast to her sentimental lover, she is, in Schiller's sense, "naive." She is unselfconscious, "natural," simple, and uncomplicated. Satisfied within her small world, she responds to Faust's passionate wooing with a directness and completeness unthinkable in a girl brought up in a higher class of society. Her charm lies in the complete absence of affectations and flirtatiousness. Her love of songs, her folk beliefs, and her immediate relationship to her traditional religion emphasize the fact that she belongs to a class in which, historically, illegitimate children were frequent and a soldier-brother felt nevertheless honor bound to denounce the villainy and attack the villain. The Gretchen story is one of the first German tragedies of the lower classes.

Goethe introduces into the searching and free world in which Faust moves Margaret's tradition-bound and limited one. When she seriously tries to win him over to her religion, he does not with the same earnestness try to imbue her with his own belief that all human beings have a common religion which cannot be designated in simple outlines or inflexible creeds (3431–58). Through his pact with Mephistopheles, Faust has left behind the prescriptive morality to which Margaret must adhere. Her love becomes tragic precisely because it ventures into a realm of standards of behavior entirely foreign to her upbringing. But, although she too has two souls, she can, within the frame of her religion, repent and be forgiven, at the same time atoning for the tragic consequences of her love—the deaths of her mother, brother, and child—by submitting to worldly justice. Within her frame of reference these are her only means of salvation. For Faust, however, repentence and forgiveness in a Christian sense are of no avail since he has left the realm of Christian thinking.

Sex and love are taken up again in the first Walpurgisnight where sex in its crassest form reigns, and the second Walpurgisnight, which is pervaded by Eros. At the beginning of the first Walpurgisnight, the roots swelling with fresh sap have sexual connotations, and the scene reaches its climax when Faust dances with a naked witch. Typically, at this moment his "higher" self asserts itself and he imagines he sees Gretchen with a narrow red band around her neck, which hints at the axe that will behead her. Compassion wins out over desire and for him the Walpurgisnight is overcome and ended. During the rest of the scene he remains completely silent.

In the Classical Walpurgisnight Faust is under the spell of Helen though he does not desire her. His best feelings are stirred by her beauty and he will, somewhat later, receive her as his queen. While he is off stage in the Netherworld to search for her, there takes place on the shores of the Aegean Sea the festival of Eros, that great ancient mythological power that holds the world together and makes it ever productive.

In contrast to the first Walpurgisnight's restless reawakening of nature in the spring, we see here a calm August night in Greece in which appear the beautiful mythological daughters of Nereus the sea-god and the sexually undeveloped Homunculus. What is displayed before us is a myth of nature in a much broader sense than that of reproduction in Spring. Sex, as presented in the Gretchen drama, remains an essential part of love, but it is ironically relegated now to Mephistopheles' hunt for the Lamiae. In the glowing beauty of Nereus' daughter Galatea, Helen is prefigured—and Galatea is given the role of Aphrodite, Eros' mother, the goddess born from the waters.

WORLDLY POWER AND ITS CORRUPTION

In the old legend Faust goes to the Emperor's court to play his tricks as a magician, his visit being one incident among many. Out of this slim plot Goethe made two acts of Part II (Acts I and IV) which, although perhaps less immediately appealing than some of the other episodes, grow on the reader who views them with regard to Faust's own development. They contain also an important statement on the realm of Mephistopheles' favorite activities—government, money, war, hypocrisy, irresponsibility, and a host of related matters—and it may be for this reason that for a scene and a half in Act I, Mephistopheles takes over and Faust does not appear. When at last Faust does appear we notice that he no longer feels the aversion to deceit that he felt in Part I, when the devil asked him to bear false witness about Marthe's husband (3040–49). On the contrary, he is now a willing accomplice who readily accepts the devil's foul means. In fact, he enjoys the magic he produces during the Masquerade scene, nor does he object, in Act IV, to Mephistopheles' three terrifying magic helpers in the war.

Whereas Faust seems to have degenerated morally, at the same time he has in some ways visibly developed. As never before, he is now a master of situations, a mature man who can dominate his environment. The fascinating fact is that this magician who produces gold only to turn it into bugs and butterflies (5590–605) is held by the court to be truly a superior figure.[16] Faust's role, in short, in these episodes is to mirror the values of his surroundings. In the home of insincerity, materialism, and frivolity, Faust simultaneously represents and exploits these characteristics. A sincere Faust would, in this environment, create a tragic situation. A Faust who plays with magic can show the court its own face.

The Emperor himself is nameless, a composite of many "Roman Emperors of the German nation," young, charming, pleasure-seeking, without a sense of responsibility. In his case, as in some other characters of the work, the symbolic function overshadows personality. He is simply *the* Emperor and his relationship to Faust remains strangely detached, although in many ways he changes Faust's destiny, as Faust changes his. He is not in any sense evil. In Act IV Faust says of him that he wishes both to govern and to enjoy himself (10251) and that this is a grave error of judgment. But it is a correct evaluation of his attitude throughout. He barely listens to his counselors' reports on the bad state of affairs in the Reich, but instead, eagerly accepts Mephistopheles' suggestion to create and produce paper money.

In Act I he shakes off his worries to participate in a Mardi Gras festival, featuring a typical Renaissance masque. The masque starts with the lowest courtiers and gradually builds up to the appearance of the Emeperor, who is disguised as the great god Pan. In the beginning female "gardeners" step forward and tell the audience that the flowers they wear are artificial, indicating, if we had any doubt, that the artificiality of the masque is intended to convey to us the artificiality of the court, which is also a kind of masquerade. And as if to make the implication doubly clear, some masquers presently appear, disguised as Graces, Fates, Furies. But their dominion shows at once that they do not understand at all the dread and serious nature of the forces they are playing and playing with—as the court does not understand its own. Instead of appearing as dread goddesses, the Fates have actually exchanged their traditional roles. The oldest, who normally cuts the thread of life, has given her scissors to the youngest and instead spins the thread. The youngest, no longer skillful in selecting the man whose life thread she will cut, has put the scissors back in their case. The middle sister, whose task is the ordering of life threads, uses the image of weaving we first heard from the Earth-Spirit. Does Goethe thereby imply that life despite all its apparent chaos is governed by some ultimate order? Or is it to emphasize the incongruity of the threads of life in the hands of a court minion?

After the allegory on Victory, Hope, Fear, and Prudence, Plutus-Faust enters in a chariot steered by the Boy-Charioteer. The latter explains that he represents poetry.[17] He has a remarkably volatile quality similar to that of the later boy-poetry figure, Euphorion, son of Helen and Faust. The allegorical relationship between poetry and Plutus, the god of wealth, is easy enough to see: Both disperse their "gold" without counting it. They can waste it because for both it is inexhaustible. As figures in the masque they are beautiful. But in the back of their chariot sits Mephistopheles disguised as Avarice. And as soon as Faust has sent Poetry back into its native solitude, he allows the crowd to catch his gold—and then turns it in their hands into ugly animals. We are back with the lowest type of witchcraft, and the grand god of wealth turns out to be an ordinary necromancer.

At this moment the god Pan appears, surrounded by mythological figures. Each sings his song, describing himself and his activities. The gnomes sing about gold and mention the ten commandments that are always broken for its sake. Later, they take the Emperor to the source of their gold, a big case that Plutus has deposited on stage. As the Emperor bends over, his beard is magically ignited. For the onlooker there is a moment of real panic, and the meaning of this *Flammengaukelspiel* becomes painfully obvious: The gold the Emperor has touched is a devouring flame. Though presented playfully, the underlying satire is serious. The Emperor will almost lose his empire in Act IV because of his lightminded handling of wealth, and he will be saved only by Faust and Mephistopheles in disguise, who will win his war for him and then leave him to his fate. In the end, he will give most of his power to the petty princes of the Reich as a reward for a victory they have not won, and will find himself in the clutches of a Church that knows better than he how to gain and hold wealth.

The disguise of Faust as Plutus, then, is an essential contribution to the implications of the work. It allows Goethe to depict every possible aspect of wealth, except its wise and equitable use, which is hinted at only in the parting lines by the court fool. But the question that the scene poses with regard to Faust's future development is a serious one. Is Goethe's treatment of the court an anticipatory mirror reflection of his hero's future actions or is it used as a contrast to them? That there exists a purposeful connection between the two scenes is evident from the fact that the land Faust ultimately owns is given to him by this same Emperor as a reward for his help

in the war. Acts I, IV, and V must therefore be regarded as a unit
interrupted by two acts devoted to antiquity and Helen of Troy.

THE GREAT REALM OF MYTH

I

THE MOTHERS AND HOMUNCULUS

The frivolous activities of the court are suddenly interrupted
and we find our imagination carried to a completely different realm.
Whereas at first sight we appear to be moving from the "real" world
of the court to the "imagined" world of myth, the truth is that we
are moving from the "un-real" activities of the court to the real
values of myth (see 6553–55). Here Faust, the participant in myth,
will shake off trickery and deceit and for the first time in his existence be the person he might ideally be. He will forget his despair
or his mockery of the illusory character of life and he will for once
be undivided and in the truest sense himself. Once again, he is
colored by the surroundings.

At the beginning of this new situation we are still at court. Faust
has put himself into the embarrassing situation of having promised
the Emperor to conjure up Paris and Helen of Troy. He therefore
pulls Mephistopheles into a "dark gallery" and asks for his help.
Mephistopheles at first tries to delay action, but then suddenly says:
"There *is* a way" (6211). The next thirty lines reveal what he calls a
"higher mystery" in tones that remind us puzzlingly of the serious-
lyrical tone of Faust. It is conceivable, as Stuart Atkins[18] assumes,
that the devil invents in these lines the "realm of the Mothers,"
creating it as he speaks; but even if this was Goethe's intention, one
cannot overlook the sudden change to lyrical language. Moreover,
Faust reacts profoundly when Mephistopheles first mentions the
Mothers. It is generally not Mephistopheles' habit to support
Faust in a serious endeavor. Here, however, both seem carried away
by Faust's anticipated trip into a realm of existence which Mephi-

stopheles describes with a verbal power otherwise reserved for Faust's great moments. The myth of the Mothers[19] is thus created before our eyes and, no matter how Mephistopheles acquired his knowledge of that realm, the reader realizes that something important is taking place. It starts with the shudder Faust experiences twice at the mention of the word "Mothers." For once he is deeply moved, and this by a name which as yet has no meaning for him. He goes even further by adding that such a shudder is "mankind's best gift":

> 'Tis not in apathy I find life's worth:
> Man's sense of awe is his best gift on earth.
> However dear he pays the world for it,
> Deep in his soul he feels the Infinite.
>
> (6271–74)

From this moment on Faust forgets the shallow world of the court, and the realm of mythic creation unfolds.

Mephistopheles introduces this realm with a description of the way to the Mothers, which to him is a way into Nothingness:

> But nothing in that ever vacant space
> You'll see, nor hear the falling of your feet,
> Nor for your tired limbs, find a seat.
>
> (6246–48)

But Faust has a premonition that here in this Nothingness he will find "all" (6256).[20] He is in a state of exultation, even before he goes to the Mothers and well before he sees Helen and falls in love with her beauty. Mephistopheles' grand words and Faust's profound excitement prepare the reader for a journey leading into the realm of creative imagination, the only world in which Faust will find not only beauty but, connected with it, the higher reality he has always yearned for. The world of myth is not distorted, as is the world of man. It carries its own truth and conviction. Faust walks into it obeying, as always, Mephistopheles' directions, not knowing what he will encounter, but sensing the uniqueness of the unknown experience.

After his return Faust ventures a full description of the Mothers and their realm, which the devil had only vaguely anticipated (6283–89).

> In your name, Mothers, in the void who dwell
> Enthroned, for ever unapproachable,
> Silent, yet friendly—round your heads there hover
> The restless forms of life which now (life over)
> Still wander, longing to perpetuate
> The sheen and glitter of the earthly state.
>
> (6427–32)

What, then, or who, *are* the Mothers? Are they Goethe's pre-Jungian version of a racial or universal memory? Everything that once existed seems to hover, shadow-like, around them in the hope of *becoming* "eternal." Hence this cannot be a realm of Platonic ideas, which have eternity by definition. The realm of the Mothers is a realm of the past—how else could Faust find Helen? The figures that move in it are "phantoms," not sunlit superior realities. And they are in a state of flux and metamorphosis. Their shadowy transformations are the "eternal pastime of the eternal Spirit," that is, their flux corresponds in some way to the flux of nature, to which the same phrase "pastime of the Spirit" might well apply. On the whole, it is probably best to call all of these figures archetypes. Faust's shudder as well as certain events concerning both Helen and Homunculus confirm such an interpretation. For both of these mythological figures the poet will have to delve into very old, far away times—for Homunculus to the beginning of evolution, for Helen to prehistoric human life.

The most beautiful woman, whatever her actual shape, is certainly an archetype. Faust had vaguely seen her in the mirror of the Witches' Kitchen, and continues to meet her throughout the work in varying shapes. The Mothers themselves, though not described and undoubtedly not "beautiful," are evidently archetypes of mankind. Their shadowy existence gives in retrospect a deepened meaning to Gretchen's motherly experiences with her little sister and her own child. The Mothers, guarding the memory of mankind, represent a more fundamental type of motherhood.

In the context of events, Faust brings back from their realm much more than the shade of Helen. The entire prehistoric world of the Classical Walpurgisnight is indirectly conjured up by his experience there. Thus, Helen can be called forth, and in the great excitement with which he has dived back into the memory of the ages, he falls in love with her shade. This is no ordinary love, but rather a precondition for his entry into myth. He is moved to the core of his existence by Helen's beauty, which makes him feel that in the realm of beauty alone lies a chance for the world to "last," to be meaningful, and in the best sense desirable.

FAUST:
> Do I have eyesight still? Have beauty's springs
> Deep in my mind been copiously revealed?
> What glorious gain my fearful journey brings!
> The world was null to me before, and sealed!
> But since my priesthood what has it become?
> First-founded, lasting, and most pleauresome!
> May all my life-strength, all my breathing fail
> If I recant or fall away from you!—
> The lovely form that once enthralled my sight
> And in the magic mirror waked delight,
> Compared with beauty such as this, turns pale!—
> I owe the impulse of all strength to you,
> And passion's very fountainhead,
> All love, all adoration—madness too.

(6487–500) (P)

These words addressed to Helen's image are the words of an artist obsessed by his vision of beauty, but they are simultaneously passionate words of love. In the entire mythological situation following these first words to Helen, their double meaning concerning both art and love will be a dominating feature. The kinship, so well known from Plato's *Symposium,* which exists in the experience of beauty with that of love, is preserved throughout. In this context Plato may be mentioned without falsification.

The moment when Faust, enamored of Helen, wants to touch her image, he sinks into a deep and long-lasting unconsciousness. Why Mephistopheles should feel that a return to Faust's old abode would help bring him back to life is never literally stated. It is implied, however, if we may assume that the devil has knowledge of any place or time where magic is being performed. Since Mephistopheles knows that Wagner is at this very moment trying to produce a man in a test tube, it follows that there must be a close connection between Homunculus, Helen, and the sleeping Faust. The help that Homunculus can give to restore Faust's consciousness lies in the fact that as a pure spirit he can read Faust's dreams and interpret them correctly. Mephistopheles is unable to do this because Faust's dreams belong to that part of his nature which is not accessible to the devil, who knows nothing about beauty and the "madness" it can create in the eye of the beholder. His lack of resourcefulness in the present crisis is furthermore due to the fact that he has no access to the world of antiquity, which preceded the medieval Christian world that created him and his myth. Nevertheless, for someone who is bewildered, Mephistopheles acts with a great deal of insight in choosing Homunculus as his helper and interpreter.

From the point of view of the economy of the play, the creation of Homunculus provides a perfect occasion to revisit Faust's old home without his ever being aware of it. The scene enables the poet to pick up the threads from the early part of the work, developing Wagner as well as the student whom the devil has earlier led astray. We realize when we see Wagner again what a limited person Faust would have become had he rejected the devil, and we are made poignantly aware of the vast contrast between his present life and his previous one. We also realize the contrast between the alchemist Wagner in his closed environment and the overpowering desire for openness and spaciousness which characterizes his creature, Homunculus, and which Faust himself will display toward the end of the work.

But the short revival of Faust's past is certainly not the only reason for Homunculus's existence. On the level of myth, he is clearly the opposite of the Mothers. They are old, ageless, and surrounded

by the shades of the past. He is new born, desirous to live, and
ready for experience. Faust is profoundly moved both by the Mothers and by the shade of Helen he brought back from them. He
barely notices Homunculus during their only brief encounter in
Act II and he will never know—nor does he care—what becomes of
his clever little guide.

Nevertheless, Homunculus is essential to the story. Though
Faust's way to the *real* Helen—as opposed to her conjured shade—
lies through the realm of nature rather than of the Mothers, there
is a dependency between the little spirit anxious to become a man
and to leave myth, and the adult man who wishes to enter the
spirit-world of myth. Unless the twofold movement from myth to
reality and from reality to myth exists, not only in the lives of
Faust and Homunculus but in the development of mankind in
general, neither myth nor nature will have the kind of "reality"
which is necessary for its acceptance by man. From the overall viewpoint of the work, the alternation between Homunculus's desire to
become man and Faust's desire to become myth is as essential a
dialectical process as Faust's own ups and downs. It is another side of
the Faust outlook, which demands that different realms of human
experience cross-fertilize.

As Faust lies in his old home in a deep sleep—sleep always produces a radical change in him—Homunculus reads in his mind the
dreamed myth of Leda and the swan. Faust does not dream of Helen
but of the moment of her conception, and Homunculus, in his in-
stinctive wish to be born, understands the process of procreation, of
becoming and growing, as it is symbolized in Faust's dream. He re-
stores Faust to life by taking him to Greece at the precise moment
of a second Walpurgisnight, another night of teeming creativity
which will see both Homunculus and Helen born in a new way.
Our last observation of Faust in this act is that he is going to Hades
to find Helen, but the Walpurgis festival of life in nature does not
permit us any doubt as to the outcome of his journey. In some
mysterious and entirely mythical way, he will be renewed, and a
real Helen, different from the shade he saw before, will be born.
Homunculus does not actually cause these events, but he symbolizes

them as he himself breaks his protective glass and, moved by love for Galatea, starts life at the beginning of time. Given the eternal recurrence of Galatea and the events of that night, he may "after millions of years" meet Galatea again—he who will grow into manhood not through the magic of Wagner, but through the benign nourishment of nature.

I have omitted so far one short but pregnant moment in the Homunculus myth. There can be no doubt that Wagner did not give life to the creature he believes to be his work. Life in the test tube starts only when Mephistopheles enters the laboratory. What Wagner believes he has achieved—namely, the creation of a human mind independent of body and sex—is an illusion. It takes the devil to create man, even though Mephistopheles does not understand that he himself represents that creative part of nature without which there would be no life. When Homunculus first sees Mephistopheles, he calls him "cousin," knowing, as a pure spirit, the real connection between Mephistopheles' actions and functions and Faust's dreams and desires. But this knowing little mind will himself prefer to go the way Faust goes, the human way of desire, impatience, and love, for this is man's lot and Homunculus is willing to accept it.

So we find almost exactly in the center of the work a myth of life which is symbolic of Faust's endeavors and elucidates them on the level of pure poetry. Faust knows less than Homunculus, but experiences more. To have given a poignant poetic life to a creature so far removed from "realistic" experience is one of Goethe's great poetic achievements.

II

Nature as Healer and Source of Life

"Nature," almost a dirty word in the eyes of modern critics, who have to face it in every eighteenth- and nineteenth-century author, varies in meaning in Faust, according to the situation in which it occurs. What the angels see on earth from their heavenly vantage point is only the senseless alternation of storms. From their overall view the details of growth and decay, of biological or physical nature are irrelevant. From Mephistopheles' viewpoint, growth and decay are absurd, useless, and stupid motions whose end, he hopes, will restore original darkness. Gretchen is never received into nature. Her protected little world has not made her aware of its existence. With Helen, as we will see, the situation is very different; her mythological existence unfolds out of the myth of the Classical Walpurgisnight and, for the time of her happiness with Faust, takes place in an idealized Arcadian landscape.

The real encounters with nature are the prerogative of Faust whose struggles to understand it are variously rewarded. He meets it first on his Easter walk during which he immediately grasps its symbolic potential: He sees the sun setting and turns it into the symbol of light and understanding by wishing to fly after it forever. He withdraws into nature after his decision to leave Margaret unharmed ("Forest and Cavern"), and has, for once, a romantic experience of nature's enveloping and protective power, his emotional union with it and the exuberance that only love can produce. The next great nature scene is the first Walpurgisnight. This is dominated by Mephistopheles and shows nature at its crudest stage of procreation. Nature is neither lovely nor soothing in this scene, but wild and oppressive. Its spaces are "vast and bare," and the "rock-noses" seem to "blow and snort" (3880). A lurid light shimmers strangely, the depth exhales vapors, and the storm-bride sweeps madly through the air.

Not much later, after Gretchen's death, we find Faust alone in a "Charming Region"—charm will be Helen's as well as Galatea's predominant feature—trying to find the peace of mind Gretchen's death has caused him to lose. The nightly nature spirits who hover around him have the power to heal him, and as the sun begins to rise Faust feels restored to a new life. He watches the sun rise, tries in vain to look into it, admires its colorful reflection in the spray of a waterfall, and takes this most fleeting of all moments—the passing rainbow created for an instant through the reflection of the sun in water—as a symbol of all life and as the essence of what man may understand of nature. The rainbow becomes "an emblem of human toil and strife" (4725); all we ever own is "the mirrored gleam" of the symbolic sun in the symbolic waterfall.

This is a rich and lovely scene; it introduces the second part of Faust and indicates, in its symbolic brevity, both nature's restorative power for man and its guidance of his mind toward an understanding of his condition.

The great nature myth of the Classical Walpurgisnight takes place almost without Faust's attention. He is so intent on finding Helen that he does not see nature around him or even the significance of the ancient nature spirits to whom he talks. In the scene on the Upper Peneios he sees these spirits in their mythological relationship to man only, and in the scene on the Lower Peneios his lovely description of the gentle river is a reflection of his earlier dream of Leda and serves only as a background for Leda's bathing companions. He rejects the nymphs' invitation to lie down to rest and instead jumps onto the back of Chiron, who leads him to Manto and the entrance of the Underworld. In contrast to Faust's normal behavior, he has no time for nature and very little interest in or patience with it. The Classical Walpurgisnight does not belong among Faust's experiences of nature.

Instead the Walpurgisnight scene has to be read on a purely symbolic level. While it presents the perfect opportunity for Homunculus to "become" (*entstehen*), this would not be enough to justify its existence in the work. I would like to suggest that, precisely because Faust is mostly absent or, if present, oblivious of his environment, Goethe could use his grand vision of nature in the center of the work to make a poetic statement on its ultimate meaning for the work as a whole. What the scene presents as Homunculus's *becoming* is also true for Faust, just as it is for man in general.

> Yield to the noble inspiration
> To try each process of creation,
> And don't be scared if things move fast;
> Thus growing by eternal norms,
> You'll pass through many a thousand forms,
> Emerging as a man at last.
>
> (8321–26)

The slow process of evolution which Thales prescribes in these words for Homunculus is man's evolutionary process in poetic form. It indicates the natural growth of man as a product of nature and emphasizes the necessity of the human position within nature. "Spirit" alone does not make man, as Faust sometimes would have wished it to do, spirit is the empty phrase Goethe mocks at in the Baccalaureus scene, and in Wagner's words on the sexlessness of Homunculus' birth. The true history of man is biological, expressed in this grand myth. It should be added that the above lines by Thales together with Proteus' speech following them abound in words which are generally applied to Faust's behavior: *wirken, regen, leben, streben* (8326–30),[21] and abundantly indicate the kinship of Homunculus and Faust. They also indicate Faust's symbolic function as a representative of "life," because these are also the essential activities of life itself.

Along with this modern myth of evolution, Goethe delves deeply into ancient nature lore. When we first accompany Mephistopheles through the realm of these "distant relatives" of his, we encounter the monsters most closely related to him. They are composed of two or three different parts, that is, they are part bird, part woman— like the sirens; or part bird, part lion, part woman—like the sphinxes. The dialogue is mocking and light. In the next scene, in which Faust in great seriousness tries to find Helen or, on the advice of the sphinxes, the old satyr Chiron who will take him to Persephone, the scenery is more beguiling and there are no monsters. Faust expatiates now on the description earlier given of his dream of Leda:

> I see where sliding waters flow
> Thro' densest brakes that scarcely stir,
> That rustle not, but whisper low;
> A hundred springs from every side
> Join in a basin deep and wide,
> A clear bright pool where bathers go.
> (7277–82)

Leda herself is invisible and we guess her existence rather than see her before us; the love scene is hidden. To be sure, even Chiron is still part animal, but he is a wise man with great healing power, and while he is as restless as any character in the work, there is sufficient time for him during his stay on the stage to inform us about his own memory of Helen and the Argonauts.

Once more we are taken back to the Upper Peneios and the obscurer monsters. In keeping with Mephistopheles' nature, an earthquake takes place, a war about gold, and other earthbound events. That part of the scene serves two functions. The first is comic relief, needed as always after a serious Faust-scene—and from many angles it is a very funny scene; the second is to introduce Homunculus to two ancient philosophers, Thales and Anaxagoras. Since Homunculus wants to *become*, two choices are offered to him. According to Anaxagoras, life is produced by volcanic action—an inadmissible theory to Goethe, which he grandly has made fun of in the sudden rising of the mountain and the subsequent war of all the greedy little monsters related to earth and metal. According to Thales, life is produced by water—a theory which draws everyone on stage who has any connection with water down to the Aegean Sea. Mephistopheles of course is left near the Upper Peneios river where he has already changed himself into Phorkias, one of the old goddesses of Fate, a form in which he will be able to serve Helen of Troy in Act III.

The last scene of the act enacts the birth of life in a symbolic myth. The participants, although water spirits, appear in human shape, indicating that the culminating point of evolution is man. Even the ever-changing Proteus, living symbol of metamorphosis, appears upon Thales' demand in "noble form" and, due to his ability to change forms, becomes the instrument for Homunculus' change into a real man. To effect this change however—which we can only surmise since it will take all the time "from the beginning of creation" (8322)—the myth of the birth of Aphrodite from the sea is presented, transformed into the radiant myth of Galatea, daughter of Nereus, who comes to visit her father every year on Walpurgisnight. Surrounded by water spirits of all kinds, she appears to her father for one brief moment—barely long enough for each to speak. But this moment, like all fulfilled moments in the work, will fill Nereus with enough happiness "to outweigh a year's monotony" (8431).

But there is much more in Galatea's appearance. In the first place she is a goddess of love and her high festival is the festival of Eros, the cosmic god "from whom all things are sprung" (8479), the god who protects fertility. In its symbolic function for the work this moment prefigures the appearance of Helen in the next act, and also the reappearance of Gretchen after Faust's death and with her the appearance of the Queen of Heaven. The Eros or love that constantly, under varying forms, creates and recreates the world appears here in a pagan vision. At the end of Act V it will appear in an equally self-created Christian myth. Homunculus, himself still hermaphroditic, finds his life now at the feet of Galatea, as Faust will find his later at the feet of Gretchen, metamorphosed into a symbol of feminine guidance.

III

HELEN OF TROY[22]

If the realm of nature ends in glory, the realm of art ends quietly and sadly. To be sure, the two young "heroes" of Acts II and III, Homunculus and Helen's son Euphorion, have much in common. Both are too radiant for this life and both are surrounded by brilliance. Both give up their living flame and "die." Faust has no relationship to Homunculus, and only a paradoxical one to Euphorion whom he tries to prevent from precisely that restlessness which is his own characteristic.

But if Euphorion has his father's curiosity he also has the volatile quality of his mother. He is far less an allegory of poetry, as is often claimed, than a fantasy of his parents, an uncontrollable, not quite real creation of two not quite real parents.

The dream quality of the third act, in contrast to the amazing "reality" of the second, is sustained from the first word to the last. Already in Act I Helen's appearance was preceded by a "cloud-like wave" (6440–50). In Faust's dream of Leda the scene ends with a

mist rising from the water and covering the love scene. After Helen
has fainted in Act III, Phorkias bids the clouds to recede so that "the
sun of this day" may reappear. When Helen and the Trojan women
walk north toward Faust's castle a mist covers them as well as the
river from which they depart. In the end Helen's clothes left behind for Faust's benefit change into a cloud that carries him away
from Greece.

We are in a realm where illusion teases reality into a kind of
pseudoreality, best characterized by the frequent question of both
Helen and Faust: Is this a dream? [23] To be sure, we are also in a
realm of beauty, as we are told quite frequently, and we witness a
"moment of existence" when Helen and Faust are united (9418).
But only five lines earlier Faust has stated that this is a dream in
which "day and place" (time and space) have disappeared. Causal
connections likewise become tenuous. We are not told how Faust
fared in Hades, or by what spirit rule Faust and Helen return to
earth at different places, or why Menelaos has been brought back.
The entire act must be accepted by the reader without his asking
why or how.

The strongest sense of unreality is given to Helen who never quite
returns to life. In the first scene her identity becomes more and more
questionable to her, until she faints and almost returns to Hades. We
witness the long suffering caused by her overpowering and dangerous
beauty. On three occasions she bewails the sufferings her beauty
once caused and each time she shudders. When she laments for the
third time, it signifies her painful farewell from Faust.

The aura of both dream and tragedy is never lifted. Helen has
borne Faust a son only to lose him and be drawn back by him to
Hades. Gretchen has loved once and come to grief; Helen has loved
often and still comes to grief. Faust's great restraint, even reticence,
in Act III and Helen's tragic beauty unite for a timeless moment
which cannot last and whose lasting quality Faust never desires.

Nowhere else in the work does Faust appear in as responsible a
position as here. He is Helen's protector—whom she urgently needs
in view of her own weakness. He is also the humble suitor and the

guiding husband just as in the last part of the act he is the responsible and loving father. Obviously, for a dream moment he is as
much removed from his "normal" self as Helen is from her self in
Hades. The two meet in an ideal world which very soon turns, at
least for a short duration, into Arcadia and the Golden Age.[24]

Nevertheless, even in this ideal realm Mephistopheles has a place.
In the guise of Phorkias he meets Helen in the deserted house of
her father, prevents her from entering her marital bedroom, and
berates her for her past sins. She counters his objections by bewail-
ing her "fate" rather than her "wrong-doing," but Mephistopheles
shakes her confidence and almost sends her back to Hades. He also
mercilessly upbraids the women in the chorus for their light-minded-
ness.

In the third scene of this act, his role becomes suddenly more
ambiguous. His description of the wide spaces of the cavern where
Euphorion was born may well be typically Mephistophelian hocus-
pocus, but his subsequent praise of Euphorion contains words we
are not used to hearing from his mouth.

And his golden lyre advancing, fashioned like a little Phoebus,
To the edge he steps serenely, to th'abyss: we stand astounded
And his parents clasp each other in the ecstasy of joy.
For what glitters round his forehead? strange the light, and hard to
    fathom;
Is it gold, or is't the effulgence of a superhuman mind?
So he moves with graceful gestures, and reveals himself thus early
As all Beauty's future master, thro' whose limbs the eternal rhythms
Flow for ever: such his nature, and as such ye too shall hear him,
And as such ye too shall see him, to your endless wonderment.

                (9622–28)

While Euphorion is on stage Phorkias-Mephistopheles says nothing,
but after Helen dies he breaks in on Faust's silence to tell him how
valuable Helen's remaining garment is.

      Tho' 'tis no more the goddess you have lost,
      Yet it is godlike none the less. Make use
      Of this inestimable favour. Rise,

And let it lift you over all things common,
Through the clear air, until you are exhausted.
(9949–53)

Did Goethe, as in Mephistopheles' first description of the way to the
Mothers, forget the devil's role because something very important
had to be said by someone other than Faust? The praise of Euphorion as the "future master of all beauty" and the emphasis on the
"divine" character of Helen's garments can hardly be called satanic.
In all three passages the voice and the choice of words is Faust's
rather than the devil's who, for all his roguishness and power of
deceit, would hardly ever be able to find this tone.

The chorus forms an interesting counterpart to Phorkias-Mephistopheles. They are Trojan women, happy to have escaped the hor-
ror of the Fall of Troy of which they remember, in a dreamlike way,
the moment when the gods walked threateningly through the flames
and the smoke. Though they are not evil, as Phorkias asserts they
are,[25] they are clearly distinguished from Helen by lack of seriousness and light-minded chatter. In the end, they are permitted to
turn into elemental spirits—dryads, oreads, naiads. But the fourth
and last group turns into protectors of the grape, and they close the
act with a wild bacchantic song, much as the satyr play closed the trio
of tragedies produced in the theatre of Dionysus. To us, it brings
a reminder of the first Walpurgisnight and so serves as a fitting
transition to Faust's return to "real life."

VICTORY AS ILLUSION

The fourth act, like the first, starts with a magnificent scene in
nature, only to be followed by a war scene considerably more ludicrous even than the court scene in Act I. Both acts have in common
the contrast between a grand natural scene in which things are
genuine and hence symbolical, and a historical scene in which things
are insubstantial and full of illusions. "Reality" is a predicate of
the realm of nature, not that of man.

At this point, as Faust returns from the mythological Arcadian
landscape, he has a glimpse of the vastness of nature which ought

to humble him. But the very opposite happens. As he sees the sea rolling uselessly to and from the shore (10211–18)—the sight reminds us of the angels' view of the meaningless storms on earth—he has, for the first time in his life, the desire to subdue it. Never before has nature inspired in Faust anything but awe and admiration. Now, back in the "real" world, he plans to dominate it. Whether this change in his attitude is to be considered good or bad will be the fundamental question we will have to ask as the play nears its end.

Faust and Mephistopheles introduce themselves to the Emperor as emissaries of a famous magician whom the Emperor once freed from the persecution of the church. Thus they are free by magic means to win for him the war against the counter-Emperor, in which he is engaged, without being recognized as his own former magicians. This freedom is needed for their ultimate purpose, which is not to help the Emperor, but to gain from him a strip of land along the sea which Faust has discovered from the mountains. It does not speak well for Faust's plans that he should gain his land by magic means and without any real concern for the Emperor's future.

In that discussion of the Emperor's war, Goethe refers three times to specific Biblical passages (Eph. 6:12; Matt. 4:8; II, Sam. 23:8). The first passage is Paul's admonition to the Ephesians that they should don their arms and fight the powerful of this earth, who rule in darkness with the evil spirits. The second is the temptation of Christ by Satan. The last tells of David's three helpers in his struggle to establish the kingdom of God. The application of these passages to the present situation is clear. The powerful of the earth, including Faust, rule here very visibly "in darkness with the evil spirits." Faust is tempted to gain a "world-dominion," which he will not, as Christ did, reject. And three aids are conjured up, destructive and greedy creatures, who will certainly not work to establish the kingdom of God. The sacrilegious irony of these passages can mean only one thing: that there will be no blessing for Faust when the land he craves to own is won.

The whole act has a destructive and frightening appearance. Nowhere is Mephistopheles so much the guiding spirit and nowhere is his magic more destructive than here. There exists a long-stand-

ing critical legend that in Part II Faust is growing and Mephistopheles is diminishing. A glance at Act IV should dispel such a notion.
Its worst aspect is that nobody, not even the Emperor, is serious
about the war. At first, the Emperor wants to fight it personally, to
prove to himself and the world that all his former jousting was
worthwhile—ludicrous behavior for a serious leader. Later, when he
deals out imperial "offices" as a reward to the "brave" fighting
princes (who have not fought seriously) the offices involve nothing
but feasting and celebrating (10873 ff). Meantime, Faust talks of
magic and Mephistopheles practices it. The high point is Mephistopheles' command to his ravens to ask the Ondines for help:

> Now my black, willing cousins, haste and take
> My greetings to the nymphs, that haunt the mountain lake,
> And beg of them the semblance of their stream;
> For they by some mysterious woman's art
> The shadow from the substance take apart,
> Until things are not what they seem.
>
> (10711–16)

When, in response, water begins to pour from the mountains,
Faust describes its disastrous effect upon the opposing army, but
Mephistopheles, in an aside to the audience, undercuts him:

> I cannot see these sham aquatic shows:
> On mortals' eyes alone they can impose.
> (10734–35)

Despite this illusion the enemy army flees. This is an insubstantial
victory for insubstantial reasons, and Goethe uses many poetic means
to turn the whole war into a farce.

The question then arises, as it did in Act I: What is the significance of this episode with regard to Faust's own kingdom? Is it
meant as a poetic contrast to the serious government of Faust? Or
is it an anticipatory mirror reflection which predicts Faust's own
behavior? The answer is not an easy one because the fifth act poses
serious problems. Only one thing seems certain: A piece of land
gained not only with the help of the devil but with so many specific
lies and so much lack of concern for the Emperor, gained, too, by

means of a farcical war and a delusion of triumph is not an achievement to be blessed.

THE WORK OF COLONIZATION AND THE END OF FAUST

The land Faust had seen from the high mountains was constantly eroded and inundated by the sea. The uselessness and senselessness of the sea's motion prompts him to wish to build dams and secure the land from the sea. This sounds useful, practical, "realistic" and, above all, unselfish. But Act V gives little support to such a view. The first scene takes place on the old dunes near the new palace which Faust has built for himself. An old couple, named after Ovid's hospitable couple, Philemon and Baucis, who have lived throughout their lives in a hut under some age-old linden trees next to a little chapel, are visited by a wanderer whom they once saved from the sea.

The idyll of their lives reminds us in language and situation of Gretchen's life before her fall. Simple, kind, hospitable, secure in their Christian faith, they enjoy an old age that seems blessed in contrast to Faust's, whose palace is uninhabited, unvisited, except by its lonely owner. Its grandeurs give him no joy. He commands and his wishes and whims are carried out, but they do not bring him satisfaction. The contrast is even stronger than the one Faust felt when he first met Gretchen; and the words he said in the Forest and Cavern scene are more than ever applicable here:

> For am I not the exiled, homeless one,
> The monster without aim or sleep.
> (3348–49)

Even though he owns a palace he is still homeless.

As he stands in his garden enviously looking at the idyllic spot before him, he craves to own it because its existence profoundly disturbs him. In a typically Faustian exaggeration he is so upset by its existence that he wishes he were "far away from here" (11162). He gives several rationalizations for his wish to own that humble property. The peal of the little church bell, called "silvery" by the guest of the old couple, irritates him and conjures up "strange shades" (11160). And the mere fact that in his vast realm this tiny property is not his turns the entire estate into nothing. The strength of his uneasiness as well as of his desire to own the place indicates that old memories are still vaguely awake in him. The ringing of the bell on that Easter night which, through its childhood associations, prevented him from committing suicide, no longer evokes happy memories, but only the uneasiness that goes with lost memories and wasted human lives. And so he orders the old couple to be removed to another place; and in the process of their removal the house catches fire and they die.

Once again, only hours before his own death, Faust becomes a criminal whose selfish desires are fulfilled at the expense of other peoples' lives. As is only fitting and just, the fire that destroys the hut of Philemon and Baucis also burns down the old trees in whose shade Faust had hoped to build a lookout. But typically and callously (Faust is however unaware that the old couple is dead), his ever restless mind imagines a lookout, built even without the lovely trees, that will permit him "to look into infinite space." We realize the contrast to his narrow room at the beginning of Part I. He behaves as in the days of his youth, filled with the strange drive that is both his curse and his salvation.

For any morally sensitive person the ease with which Faust moves from regret to new desire is shocking. And this is undoubtedly Goethe's intention. Just as Faust enjoyed the climb up the Brocken mountain during the Walpurgisnight, having killed Gretchen's brother and deserted her only hours earlier, so he enjoys here the thought of that free view into the distance almost at the moment of the destruction of the old place. Even now his vitality for new experience is considerably greater than his regret, which has barely any moral quality to recommend it. When, a moment later, Mephistopheles informs him of the old people's death, his only response is to curse his helpers. But the incident cannot be so easily dismissed. Care (*Sorge*), the one human attitude he had rejected in his youth, finds entrance into his palace as a magical figure.

Faust had rejected Care for the first time right after the Earth-Spirit appeared to him and left him in despair (644–51). At that moment he described it as the tie that binds a man to his environment—possessions, wife, children—anything that causes him to worry and robs him of his own initiative. Again, just before entering the pact with Mephistopheles (1583–606) he cursed everything that ties a man down—a comprehensive curse which makes him precisely the lonely wanderer he turns out to be. As a result of this curse, he has been free from human bonds and, until recently, from possessions. But he has also been excessively lonely, a man without responsibility, without unselfish love, without consideration for others, precisely a man without Care.

Now Care talks to him in a strange singsong. She does not mention Philemon and Baucis, but their senseless death clearly justifies her presence. Faust once again repudiates her power, and angrily she blinds him. It takes Faust just one line to become reoriented to his old habits in his new blindness. "But deep within a radiant light now burns," (11500) he says, and an inner vision takes the place of his previous desire for a spacious view, which had been the strongest motive for his wish to remove the cottage of Philemon and Baucis.

Symbolic of both the desire to see and the grief that "seeing" may cause is Lynceus' song at the beginning of this scene. It starts with the happiness of seeing and ends in grief:

> Thus see I how all things
> In beauty are dressed:
> And all things delight me,
> Myself with the rest.
> O fortunate eyes,
> Whate'er ye have seen
> Whate'er may befall you
> How fair it has been!
> (11296–304)

But a few lines later when he discovers the fire, he says:

> Must my eyes such sights be sharing?
> Must my vision be so clear?
> (11328–29)

The gift of powerful eyesight is, like all human gifts, ambiguous.

Certain qualities of Faust are brought out strongly in these short, but highly symbolic scenes. He is never passive, suffering, or willing to accept the fate that befalls him. Instead, his vitality drives him on to new "acts," even though he is a hundred years old and new blows are sure to be forthcoming. He needed the nature spirits at the beginning of Part II to soothe his conscience after Gretchen's death. In Act V he pushes this conscience aside with two angry lines to Mephistopheles. And even when the real personal affliction of physical blindness strikes him, he gives it not a thought. Care has indeed no hold on him.

Before Care enters his room Faust expresses for the only time in the poem the desire to be rid of the spirit world:

> Could I the powers of magic ban,
> Have done with spells and sorcery,
> Stand before Nature merely as a man,
> Then life would have its worth again for me.
>
> (11404–407)

But there would be no play, no hero, no desire, no rest if his wish were granted. He is wrong to recoil from the magic in his path. The demonic forces *are* life, his life. Without his pact with Mephistopheles and his awareness of the existence of the demonic world, he would not have become "human," in the full sense in which Wagner for example can never follow him.

The importance of the fact that Care as a human attitude is rejected by Faust once and for all can hardly be overemphasized. Care means the responsibility for others even if this is a burden; it means human bonds even if they are felt as bonds; it means protection not only for others but for oneself. What gives value to life for most people, namely human relationships and the care for possessions, was rejected by Faust when he made his pact with the devil. Faithful to the latter, he has kept his word. No one except the devil has been his companion through life, and possessions have not mattered to a man who disposes of magic means. Now he owns land, but he has not learned the lesson of Care, and people die through his greed.

His possessions are not only ill-begotten, they are also badly handled. Baucis describes to the guest the nightly work of the demonic helpers:

> Nightly echoed tortured screams,
> Such as bleeding victims raise;
> Seawards flowed the fiery streams,
> Turned by day to waterways.
> (11127–30)

She has the same instinct Margaret had when she sensed the presence of Mephistopheles, and while her description may be exaggerated by her suspicions, we feel that she is basically right.

Only two pages later Mephistopheles describes the piracy by which he and the three powerful helpers have acquired the treasures they are bringing to their master:

> Here nothing helps but power to snatch:
> We catch a fish, a ship we catch:
> And if of three we're quickly master,
> We hook the fourth one all the faster.
> The fifth one's chances then are slight;
> And all is well, since might is right.
> One thinks of "what" and not of "how",
> And I'm no sailor, that I vow,
> Unless war, trade, and looting be
> An indivisible trinity.
> (11179–88)

Faust has become constitutionally incapable of considering these evils. He grandly disregards his servants because, while he does not care about wealth, he also does not care about the wickedness that may be the foundation of its acquisition. Neither the nightly magic of canalization nor the vicious plunderings of other men's possessions are able to attract his attention. Is this, then, as always in his life, the negative side of some positive action? Most Faust scholars feel that this is so. They feel that his colonizing work, the act of building dams and digging canals, is his service to humanity, and that this, like almost every human action, carries with it dubious behavior and may be founded on evil deeds.

Against this widespread opinion a number of objections can be raised. Nowhere is mention made of human beings for whose sake Faust is carrying out his plans.[26] Instead, we hear only of his personal whims to prevent the sea from inundating the country. The only human beings mentioned anywhere are those who are killed. Not a sign of life is felt around his lonely palace, apart from the demonic helpers and the very lonely voice of Lynceus, who soon changes his song from praise of the world and its beauty to lamenting over the fire and its destruction of the linden trees.

This situation, together with Faust's rejection of Care, seem clear indications that Faust's work of land reclamation cannot lay claim to moral value. On the contrary. This is Faust's latest hubris in a life filled with it. He who has always been reverent toward nature now seeks to dominate it. He does not give a thought to there being people in "his" realm, which he calls a "world-empire" (11241). In this speech, more than in any other of the entire work, Faust's self-centeredness emerges from every line. *I* want the trees, he says to Mephistopheles, for they are not now *mine; I* want to see all *I* have done, "the human spirit's masterpiece" (11248). There is here no room for Care, no trace of humility, no sense whatever of service to one's fellow human beings. On the contrary, the man who could once feel as part of nature, in fact a humble part, is now trying to subdue nature, and fails.

The misinterpretation of Faust's last deeds as constituting a service to humanity must partly be explained by a real misreading of the text in the nineteenth century, which believed so firmly in the value of colonization. It is also partly due, I believe, to the difficulty which arises when one has to face Faust's ultimate "salvation." It is hard to see a man saved who has never done anything to deserve redemption. And yet this entirely undeserved salvation is what Goethe tries to show, as we will see in a moment.

The time of the action is now "Deep Night" (starting 11288), "Midnight," and the interval before dawn.[27] Faust's life ends, as it began, at night. If this has any symbolic significance—and one can hardly doubt that it does—it can mean only that no deeper insight is given to him now than before. Since the day-night symbolism is so pervasive throughout, there is no reason to assume that Goethe suddenly became negligent. On the contrary, the night scenes make an unmistakable negative statement on Faust's last hours.

Goethe's ironic touch is again active here, for Faust dies under an illusion, the greatest of all. The entire death scene is farcical. The Roman lemures[28] sing comic songs reminiscent of the graveyard scene in *Hamlet,* Mephistopheles puns on *Graben* and *Grab*,[29] and Faust himself mistakes the sound of the shovels digging his grave for the ones he had ordered to finish the last canal. For the first time in his life his great intelligence, always fed through his eyes, is misguided. He enjoys the sound of the shovels which, he believes, will reconcile the earth with itself, set a limit to the waves, and dam in the ocean (11540–43). But in all this he is deluded. Then suddenly comes a different vision. For the first time in his entire life he sees the good his work might do for others, a "paradise" on earth, in which "millions" of people could live "actively free." He would like to stand with such free people on a free soil and reconquer this freedom with them from day to day:

> Then to the moment I could say
> "Remain! remain! thou art so fair!"
> The traces of my earthly day
> In aeons shall not disappear.
> And so, in foretaste of that bliss divine,
> This last, transcendent moment now is mine.
>
> (11581–86)

He has pronounced the words of the pact and dies. Obviously, these words do not fulfill the covenant—fulfillment remains in the *conditional* (subjunctive mood in German). The last canal will never in fact be built: "Old Neptune, the water-devil," in Mephistopheles's words, will destroy all that Faust has begun. The irony is thus profound and disturbing but entirely appropriate to the life of a man who ran from illusion to illusion.

That Faust should be redeemed on the basis of one grand dream which will not materialize is a tenuous assumption, made, however, by some critics who want to hold on to something positive. But how positive is a dying man's last vision, especially when he is made to speak of "millions of people" and "eons of time" as though they were in his power? I find Goethe's irony at this point as crushing as Faust's hubris, and I cannot attribute anything but a characterizing value to the dream, which shows the usual self-indulging posturing of Faust's egotism. It is also fair, I think, to consider the evidence of Mephistopheles. We cannot discount his comments here or elsewhere; they must never be excluded, although they are never totally true. Mephistopheles's epitaph for Faust is:

> No pleasure sates him, nor no joys suffice:
> In vain he grasps at shapes that ever shift;
> Till now the poor fool craves t'immortalise
> The last poor empty moment that is left.
>
> (11587–90)

Knowing Faust, we may well wonder whether, had he finished his work, he would indeed have tolerated "a free people on a free soil." Something, we suspect, would have crossed his good intentions, as so often previously, and he would have turned to other "shapes that ever shift." The illusory vision, then, does not indicate a change of heart, but rather one more self-deception. This conclusion is confirmed by the fact that, despite the literal loss of the bet, Faust actually wins it and the devil will not get his soul. For Mephistopheles to win, Faust would have to linger over something he loved. This he has never in fact done. Even his dream of a paradise on earth (undercut by his own egoism) is transient, and his sentence with its conditional: "Then to the moment I *could* say . . ." is an insubstantial thing. *Faust*, the play, and Faust, the character are consistent from the first line to the last, and Goethe's assumption of the passing quality of all earthly things is adhered to without wavering.

To make Faust's winning of the pact entirely clear Goethe introduces, immediately following Faust's death, a farcical scene. The mouth of hell is placed on the stage to receive Faust's soul, as at the end of the puppet play versions of the tale. But here matters turn out differently. Angels appear and scatter rose petals to spread love among the satanic group. Slyly they wait until Mephistopheles's attention is averted by a handsome boy-angel, then they seize Faust and carry his "immortal part" upward. They have hoodwinked Mephistopheles as he has been accustomed to hoodwink human beings; he is treated as he liked to treat others and the joke is on him. And though he rightly complains that he has wasted a great effort, and we must agree that his many years of untiring service to Faust bring him no reward, we must also recall that, preferring "the living over the dead" he willingly agreed to Faust's terms for the bet and helped him considerably even if unintentionally to keep its terms. The comedy of the scene makes it impossible for the audience to sympathize with his loss, and as he leaves we laugh at him.

The Meaning of Faust's Life and It's Function in the Work

The final scene, entitled "Mountain Gorges," restates in short form most of the poem's concerns. It is obviously meant to be a statement, if not on Faust's character, at least on the meaning of his life. Rarely in the work do we find such tension between things actually said and their symbolic significance. Goethe puts before us a grand tableau of saints distributed over mountainous slopes, from the center of which arise, first, the souls of innocent children who have died during birth, and a little later, angels, who carry Faust's immortal part. All of this, the whole scene before us, including the mountainsides, is in motion. The rising groups of souls are met from above by the Queen of Heaven surrounded by repentant sinners, among them Gretchen. As they meet the boys and angels, they turn upward, followed by those who have just left the earth, and a Mystical Chorus is heard to sing:

> Everything passing
> is only a symbol.
> (12104–105)

The scene itself resembles a late Renaissance painting. The contrast between the dark mountainsides and the various groups, seen as clouds which rise and descend in the center, evokes distinct impressions of sixteenth- or seventeenth-century apotheoses. There are furthermore strong reminiscences of Dante. The conception of newborn dead and the prayer of Doctor Marianus (Saint Bernard) derive from the *Divine Comedy*, and there are references to the Bible as well. What are we to make of all this?

Before discussing the details, the ironic light this scene sheds on the entire work needs to be examined. Both Faust and Mephistopheles have made a pact valid on earth only. In the Pact scene Faust shrugs off the Beyond by saying it does not concern him (1660), and as late as the scene with Care he states that man cannot look beyond earth. The assumption that there is no hereafter and that this life is all he has is largely the curse of Faust's restlessness. No life could be called more earthbound than Faust's. Was this a grand deception? There is furthermore great irony in the fact that Gretchen, whom he deserted in her misery, is now guiding him, indicating a way "upward" of which he is not yet aware. In an utterly unforeseeable manner his wish for an "eternity" of their love has come true.

At the same moment, the irony of the whole gives way to a serious and hymnic tone. The joy and love that Faust never felt before are suddenly present. Why, then, we must ask, did Faust have to undergo the pain of his life: Why could he not have reached his present state through suicide, as he intended to? There is a profound clash in the juxtaposition of this fulfillment with the restless disappointments we have witnessed for so long. Are the latter invalidated by the former?

Hardly. For it seems clear that unless Faust were to live his total life, the last scene could never come about. If it has a message, it is that the totality of life has to be endured before any kind of salvation is possible. The "blessed boys" state that Faust has "learned" and therefore can teach them, they who have not lived. Thus the emphasis of the scene is still on life, growth, striving. While we are no longer within the confines of mortal life, we are very far from anything resembling heaven. Faust stands at the very beginning of a process of metamorphosis of whose ultimate shape we know nothing. There is still a "remnant of earth" in him and he is far from being pure spirit. He is at the "chrysalid stage," and we will not see the butterfly. In fact, his salvation holds no promise for anyone outside the poem. It does not express a doctrine, barely anything approaching faith. It is the presentation of a potential afterlife which is almost a continuation of mortal life—a life in which Faust's "immortal part" will grow and change and rise upward toward eternal love.

At this point, a few words of warning are in order. The scene's Christian exterior should not be taken to imply Christian salvation —the complete absence of Christ, even of the mention of His name, argues against this assumption. Similarly, the Penitent Women do not prefigure penitence on the part of Faust.[30] Goethe chose some well-known presentations of afterlife to convey through them, symbolically, what he himself calls the "inexpressible." He leans heavily on Dante's Queen of Heaven, just as he had leaned on the Book of Job in the Prologue. He uses Mary as a myth, similar to the myth of Galatea and the myth of Helen. Since myth-making is the strength of the poem, the Christian myth of the afterlife is as fitting as any other. We must be warned, too, against taking the word "salvation" literally. *Faust* is not a drama of redemption. It contains no Savior and has no need for one. If we speak on the symbolic level, indeed, it contains no devil. Mephistopheles acts out the role of a Christian devil, but playfully, jokingly. He poses as the devil because this gives him unending chances to revile the Church and the priesthood. Symbolically, however, as we saw earlier, he simply represents all that is unspiritual in life, everything that binds man to earth. It is on this account that he can be made into such a rich, varied, and live character. He is "evil" only in the sense that his empire includes the darker instincts of man, and he is a nihilist only in the sense that he negates the value, even the existence of spirituality.

With all this in mind, the meaning of Faust's salvation becomes intelligible. Goethe goes very far in making Faust guilty because he wants to demonstrate that Faust's salvation is independent of either repentance or good works, that Faust is saved because he has *lived,* not because he has become a good man. Goethe writes an un-Christian play with a deceptively Christian ending. But the ending is not in fact more Christian than the rest. The play is consistently un-Christian and Faust's salvation has nothing to do with Church dogma. From a strictly religious point of view the last scene might be considered blasphemous, because the saving of this particular soul goes against all Christian principles.

Perhaps the last scene has escaped religious criticism because it is so essentially aesthetic. Once more we find ourselves in nature, in "Forest, Rocks, Solitude." Once more the seemingly steady landscape is in motion:

> Forests they wave around:
> Boulders they load the ground:
> Tree-roots they coil and cling
> Tree-stems in masses spring
> (11844–47)

—with a motion in which all on stage participate, as in Baroque art.

The dark fir trees shelter a "morning cloud," which gradually turns out to be the souls of "innocent boys," moving gradually and solemnly from the dark region of the Anchorites into the central light toward which the Mater Gloriosa is descending.

But the picturesque quality lies only partly in this Landscape with Figures. It is present too in the language (unhappily this cannot be sensed in the translation), in the last manifestation of the symbolism of darkness and light, in the swelling tones of love and gladness which we hear for the first time. The liberation of the mind from the "bond of the senses" and the "rough paths of the earth" is celebrated here with great relief by a poet who, up to now, has given his best powers to the presentation of those paths. Now, happy and loving as he never was in life, Faust may lay down the human burden.

At the same time we realize that the background of neo-Platonic thought on which Goethe habitually drew is again making itself felt. If there is a world-soul, as neo-Platonism maintained, and if man's immortal part is destined to return to it from the misery of this earthly existence, then this is the process we see beginning to take place. Hemmed in by the mountainous slopes and lighted only in the center and from above, the continually shifting landscape of the last scene affords a symbol of Faust's whole life as it runs its course in a vale of darkness lit only, but always, by some incomprehensible ray of light. In a way, too, the last scene proposes possibilities other than the earthly ones that we have actually witnessed. Though the human tragedy ends with death, somewhere within the wide scope of the world-soul's manifestations lies the mystic return of everything created to the source whence it came. This cannot be considered a happy ending of the poem itself because it lies outside of it. And it happens only after the disappearance of Mephistopheles. What is suggested is a potential continuation of life in some form of spiritualized essence, a life in which good and evil no longer exist, and past good and evil are accepted because they are an integral part of the earthly lot. Whoever has fully subjected himself to life on earth, Goethe seems to imply, may continue to live in spirit.

Neither the Lord nor Mephistopheles understands fully the sublimation that takes place here. New possibilities open up unknown to the actors of the play. Faust never suspected them because the "light of Heaven," whose presence he vaguely felt while "eating dust," failed to "reveal" itself, as a Christian light might have been expected to do. This "light" is, in some sense, the ultimate source of Faust's restlessness. We know of its presence, however, only because it is for Faust at moments a felt truth. Even in the end, it is revealed only symbolically, cautiously, altogether as a poetic image which indicates a direction, not a reality. If we leave Faust in happier climes we do so only through poetry. The sublimity of Goethe's parting words may be a promise for Faust within the poem, but they are not for the author, who necessarily remains outside the world he has created. Perhaps their office is to help us leave that world without despair. Their soothing beauty is the light an artist can shed over the dark life of a man whose evil doing, solitude, despair, and disappointed aspirations we will not easily forget.

CHRONOLOGY

1749	Birth of Johann Wolfgang von Goethe in Frankfurt on August 28.
1759	Frankfurt is occupied by the French during the Seven Years War (1756–63).
1765–68	Studies in Leipzig.
1768–70	Stay in Frankfurt.
1770	Studies in Strasbourg.
1771	Publication of *Goetz von Berlichingen.*
1772	Stay in Wetzlar, location of *The Sorrows of Young Werther.*
1773–75	Frankfurt. Publication of *Werther.* Beginning of *Faust.*
1775	Goethe is invited to court by the Duke of Weimar. Moves to Weimar where he resides the rest of his life.
1786–88	Travels in Italy. Publication of *Iphigenie, Egmont, Tasso.*
1790	First edition of collected works in 8 volumes; includes the *Fragment* of *Faust.*
1791	Takes over the direction of the theatre.
1794–1805	Close friendship with Schiller; joint publications.
1796	Publication of *Wilhelm Meister's Apprenticeship.*
1805	Schiller dies.
1808	Collected works in 12 volumes; contains *Faust,* Part I.
1809	Publication of *The Elective Affinities.*
1811–22	Works on his autobiography.
1815–19	Second edition of collected works in 20 volumes.
1816	Death of his wife.

1819 Publication of *The West-Eastern Divan*.
First performance of parts of *Faust* in Berlin.

1826–31 Complete edition of his works, continued after his death.
Faust, Part II published 1833.

1832 Death in Weimar on March 22.

✧ NOTES ✧

1. This is the so-called *Urfaust,* rediscovered by the Germanist Erich Schmidt in 1887.

2. George Santayana, *Three Philosophical Poets* (1910).

3. This question of the reality behind the dream ceases to exist when, in Part II, Faust has entered the realm of Poetry. His dream of Leda and the swan (6903–17) foreshadows the poetic reality of his meeting with Helen of Troy.

4. See Ernst Loeb, *Die Symbolik des Wasserzyklus bei Goethe* (Paderborn: Schoeningh Verlag, 1967).

5. See Wilhelm Emrich, *Die Symbolik von Faust II* (Bonn: Athenäum Verlag, 1957), mainly Chap. 1.

6. Thus Anaxagoras' invocation of "Diana, Luna, Hecate" is condemned through the subsequent events:

> Hear then, Eternal one, ever the same,
> Thou of the triple form, the triple name;
> Now in my people's need, I call to thee,
> Diana, Luna, Hecate!   (7902–905)

This is a mythological trinity that borders on the satanic because Hecate is the goddess of the Underworld and deals in magic. Quite another type of trinity is mentioned in line 11188.

7. This does not contradict the earlier statement that *Faust* is a work dealing with scientific concepts. The question is simply one of levels. Scientific and mythological views reinforce rather than contradict each other. The same observation is valid with regard to the mythological realm of magic.

8. See, for example, most of the Herald's speeches in Part II, Act I.

9. See Harold S. Jantz, *Goethe's Faust as a Renaissance Man: Parallels and Prototypes* (Princeton University Press, 1951).

10. "Gothic" in the usage of the time includes the Renaissance period.

11. On a literal level Lynceus is not the identical character in Act III and Act V, but the literal level is unimportant here and he maintains in both places his symbolic-human identity.

12.
> *Tätig ihn Preisenden,*
> *Liebe Beweisenden,*
> *Brüderlich Speisenden,*
> *Predigend Reisenden*
>
> For you as you praise Him,
> Proving your love
> Fraternally sharing,
> Preaching and faring
> (801–804) (P)

In the German original, all four lines rhyme on their last three syllables, a feat not easily accomplished in translation.

13. This scene is discussed in greater detail under Myth II below.

14. The entire passage reads as follows:

> In tides of life, in action's storm
> I surge as a wave,
> Swaying ceaselessly;
> Birth and the grave,
> An endless sea,
> A changeful flowing,
> A life all glowing:
> I work in the hum of the loom of time
> Weaving the living raiment of godhead sublime.
> (501–509) (P)

15. In this scene, after greeting the drinking students, Faust remains an entirely silent observer until he blurts out: "Might we not now proceed upon our way?" (2296). Drinking is never mentioned again except at the end of Act III. Faust is not the character to drown himself in drink.

16.
> True worth no words can fitly grace:
> Still—here's a healthy moonlike face:
> Lips that are ripe, cheeks full of round,
> By the bejewelled turban crowned;
> A gathered robe, for easy wearing:
> But how can I describe his bearing?
> Some mighty lord he seems to be.
> (5562–68)

17. The German text, which echoes some of its own words, has a peculiarly poetic quality:

> *Bin die Verschwendung, bin die Poesie;*
> *Bin der Poet, der sich vollendet,*
> *Wenn er sein eigenst Gut verschwendet.*
> (5573–75)

I am Profusion, I am Poesy:
The Poet who fulfils himself, when he
Gives forth his inmost soul unstintedly.

18. Stuart Atkins, *Goethe's Faust* (Cambridge: Harvard University Press, 1958), pp. 133–141.

19. See Harold Jantz, *The Mothers of Faust* (Baltimore, Johns Hopkins Press, 1969).

20. The German word *All* can mean the entire universe or it can apply to an individual, as in "you are my all, my everything."

21. These words do not appear clearly enough in the Shawcross translation. *Wirken,* etymologically related to the English "work," means "to act, to *effect.*" (It is also said of the Earth-Spirit.) *Regen* means "to move" and *streben* "to strive." This passage, perhaps more clearly than any other, shows the meaning of "striving" to be identical, in Goethe's usage, with "living," "acting," "moving," even "changing."

22. Neither the Classical Walpurgisnight nor the Helen act takes place in what we generally call classical antiquity. Goethe goes to some length to dispel such a notion. Not only are the mythological figures, including Phorkias, much older than the Homeric age (see, for example, 7197–98), but both the Doric temple in front of which Helen's shade first appears (6403–14) and Menelaos' palace with its Cyclopean walls (9018–21) are purposely contrasted with the much more elegant Gothic style and are made to appear archaic rather than classical.

23. For example, see lines 8837–40 and 8880–81.

24. It is ironic that Faust's description of the ideal life in untouched nature (9526–61), given before the scene changes to Arcadia, does not correspond to the events and the setting of the latter. His description is a literary convention, whereas the real scene which follows is a successful, typically Faustian, and above all tragic scene.

25. Who are ye then, that thus before the palace gates
Ye like demented drunken Maenads, rave and rage?
Who are ye then, that thus ye dare to howl against
The house's guardians, like to dogs that bay the moon?
Dream ye, I know not what your race nor whence ye spring?

Ye war-engendered, battle-nurtured, half-grown brood,
Lustful, seducing even as ye are seduced,
Who sap the strength of soldier and of citizen,
When thus in crowds I see you, 'tis as though I saw
A swarm of locusts settling on the new-sprung grain.
Devourers of another's labours! ye that suck
And drain the fruits of hardly-won prosperity.
Wares without value, looted, bartered, bought and sold.

(8772–83)

26. The only exception occurs in Faust's very last speech, which will be discussed below, in which people are, although not present, at least envisioned as part of his future plans. See also the very brief hint at a potential population, lines 11249–50.

27. That it is still dark is clear from the stage direction, "Torches" (11511).

28. In Roman mythology, lemures were night-walking spirits of the dead that haunted the living in a restless, frightening way.

29. "The German words for "ditch" and "grave" are both derived from the verb *graben* ("to dig").

30. They specifically pray for Gretchen (12065–68).

◄§ BIBLIOGRAPHY ℰ►

IN ENGLISH

Atkins, Stuart, *Goethe's Faust: A Literary Analysis.* Cambridge: Harvard University Press, 1958. A detailed running commentary, based on extensive scholarship not only on Goethe but also on ancient and other sources used by him. Although somewhat heavy reading and criticized for some bold interpretations, the book presents the most thorough, perceptive analysis in English, or perhaps in any language. One may disagree with individual statements, but will always find the book helpful and stimulating.

Fairley, Barker, *Goethe's Faust: Six Essays.* Oxford University Press, 1953. This is a classic book in the sense that it has outlasted other critical works. It presents intelligently and with great sensitivity some of the main problems concerning the work.

Gillies, Alexander, *Goethe's Faust: An Interpretation.* New York: The Macmillan Company, 1957. Written expressly for the English-speaking undergraduate, it gives the factual details of the story. An invaluable introductory guide; lucid, consistent, and backed by a profound knowledge of the subject-matter.

Jantz, Harold, *Goethe's Faust as a Renaissance Man: Parallels and Prototypes.* Princeton University Press, 1951. A fascinating study of many sources of *Faust,* mainly occult. Elucidates some of the more difficult and obscure passages of the work.

————, *The Mothers in Faust.* Baltimore: Johns Hopkins Press, 1969. A study of ancient and Renaissance imagery related to the Mothers episode. Fascinating reading, especially for those interested in iconography.

Vickery, John B. and J. Sellery, eds., *Goethe's Faust Part One: Essays in Criticism*. Belmont, Calif.: Wadsworth Publishing Co., Inc. 1969. A very useful collection of essays by the best known Faust scholars of today, including some original translations from German essays, judiciously edited in order to concentrate on *Faust I*. An aid to understanding individual passages, the book is also helpful in exploring the larger aspects of *Faust* criticism. Contains a bibliography which indicates various facets of the vast amount of Faust scholarship.

In German

Emrich, Wilhelm, *Die Symbolik von Faust II. Bonn: Athenäum* Verlag, 1957. The most authoritative German study on the symbolism in Part II. Although heavy-handed and difficult, its consistent interpretation of symbols as they appear in clusters and layers is most instructive. Invaluable for a thorough study of the work.

Goethes Werke. Hamburg: Christian Wegner Verlag. Volume III (first published in 1949, with many reprints since) contains the critical edition of *Faust,* together with excellent notes and introductions by Erich Trunz.

May, Kurt, *Faust II. Teil, in der Sprachform gedeutet*. Munich: C. Hanser, 1962. (Originally published 1936.) A rewarding and thorough investigation of the poetic language of Part II, showing the degree to which an interpretation of the work must depend on Goethe's choice of words, rhymes, meters, etc.